Library of
Davidson College

THE FIRE FLARES ANEW

A Look at the New Pentecostalism

by
JOHN STEVENS KERR

FORTRESS PRESS
Philadelphia

To Joanne, David, Kirsten, and Sean,
whose love must be a gift of the Spirit.

Biblical quotations from the New English Bible, copyrighted 1961 and 1970, by the Delegates of the Oxford University Press and the Syndics of the Cambridge University Press, are used by permission.

COPYRIGHT © 1974 BY FORTRESS PRESS

All rights reserved. No part of this publication may be reproduced, stored in a retrieval system, or transmitted in any form or by any means, electronic, mechanical, photocopying, recording, or otherwise, without the prior permission of the copyright owner.

Library of Congress Catalog Card Number 73-89061

ISBN 0-8006-1074-1

4064K73   Printed in the United States of America   1-1074

TABLE OF CONTENTS

ONE	PENTECOST AGAIN	1
TWO	WHERE IT ALL BEGAN	8
THREE	THE FIRE DIES	26
FOUR	THE FIRE FLARES ANEW	39
FIVE	THE FIRE SPREADS	47
SIX	WHAT IS PENTECOSTALISM?	63
SEVEN	THE GIFTS: GOD'S OR MAN'S?	82
EIGHT	WILL THE FIRE BUILD OR BURN?	96

CHAPTER ONE

PENTECOST AGAIN

The conservative Church of Christ recently kicked out one of its most illustrious and dedicated families—the Pat Boones. What ghastly scandal forced the Church of Christ to disown this fine, all-American family?

Simply this: they spoke in tongues.

Tongues, or *glossolalia*, to use the technical biblical Greek term, are a kind of speech uttered by Christian believers under the influence of the Holy Spirit. Though tongues sound similar to an Oriental or Scandinavian language in their tone, they are actually unintelligible. Speakers in tongues claim that the gift of tongues is one of the special gifts of the Holy Spirit—along with prophecy, healing, and some others—which is available to "fulfilled" Christians.

The movement that centers around these special gifts of the Holy Spirit is called the Pentecostal movement. It traces its history, and takes its name, from the events described in Acts 2. There we read that, on the occasion of the Jewish festival of Pentecost, the apostles first spoke in tongues as the Holy Spirit came upon them. Pentecostals believe that their "Spirit baptism," which is evidenced by their ability to display the "gifts of the Spirit," is the same "baptism" as the one the disciples received on that first Pentecost. Thus they stand in a direct line of succession to the earliest, apostolic church.

There are three kinds of Pentecostalism existing today. Each variety shares much with the others, but there are important differences we shall note from time to time. Their main common element is celebrating and manifesting the gifts of the Holy Spirit. Under this broad umbrella, we can distinguish the traditional or classic Pentecostals, the Catholic Pentecostals (or Catholic charismatics, as they are sometimes referred to—*charisma* being a Greek word meaning "gifts"), and the neo-Pentecostals. This last group is made up of those in the main line denominations who have embraced the Pentecostal experience in recent years.

Today, these groups comprise what is probably the fastest growing and most controversial movement in the Christian church.

The growth of Pentecostalism has been phenomenal. Consider these facts:

—Traditional Pentecostals report over two million members in North America alone.

—Worldwide, the movement counts twenty million adherents.

—While regular denominations stand still or decline, the Pentecostal denominations grow at an amazing rate.

—The fastest growing form of Christianity in the Third World—especially in Latin America and Africa—is Pentecostalism.

How could all of this happen in the world of Christianity without the vast majority taking notice? The answer: Pentecostalism moved along the soft underbelly of society where the middle and upper middle class church people never traveled.

When it began, Pentecostalism belonged to the hill people of Kentucky, the black and white sharecroppers, the dirt farmer, and the urban poor. They met in store fronts and claptrap country churches. Many of their clergy lacked a high school diploma. And their worship, filled with emotion and shouting, surely missed the standards of middle class decorum.

Sociologists in the universities and regular church people with interests in peculiar forms of Christianity studied Pentecostalism from time to time. They generally concluded that it was the religion of the oppressed and the poor. Its emotion filled a vacuum in their impoverished lives; its promise of supernatural spiritual gifts compensated its people for their lack of worldly wealth. While they held to some strange doctrines (that is, doctrines which sounded absurd to the minds of clergy trained in universities and seminaries), they might be forgiven. After all, poor people need something, and we shouldn't be too critical of our less educated brothers.

This basically paternalistic view prevailed for some time. Perhaps a lot of main line churchgoers were secretly grateful to the Pentecostals. So long as these people served the poor blacks and poor whites, the main line people didn't have to bother themselves with such people.

The first notice that Pentecostalism was a serious movement which could not be treated in so dilettante a fashion came from overseas, especially Latin America. The Roman church—and the few Protestant churches—in this nominally Christian continent suddenly noted that millions who would have nothing to do with their churches flocked to the Pentecostal groups. Again, they were the poor and the oppressed, but in Latin America such people are the masses, rather than a minority. Established churches in Latin America were identified in the eyes of the people with the oppressive upper classes.

Suddenly, scholars began to think of Pentecostalism in political and class terms. Could it be a religious "protest movement"? Since it appealed to the same social classes the revolutionaries worked on, might it represent a political threat to the established order? Or did it represent a protest of another kind?

No one had certain answers for these questions, but all agreed on one point: any movement which grew this fast could not be ignored. Theologians who observed the world Christian scene began to speak of Pentecostalism as the "third force" in Christianity, along with Protestantism and Roman Catholicism.

Shortly after the churches in the Third World awakened to the giant in their midst, the churches of North America discovered the same thing. The intrusion of Pentecostalism into the main line churches happened so fast, and so suddenly, many Christians were caught unawares. What is this thing? How did it begin? What does it mean? These questions suddenly became terribly important. So long as a Pentecostal worshiped in the church down the road, he could be ignored. But when your friend in the next pew calls himself a Pentecostal—and a Presbyterian as well—the problem comes directly home.

When the movement spread into conventional churches beginning in the early 1960s, it grew at a rate not often seen in religious circles. Right now, estimates of the number of neo-Pentecostals and Catholic charismatics run between five hundred thousand and one million. Well-known figures in the established churches admit to speaking in tongues. "Prayer fellowships" and "Spirit fellowships"—the small groups in which the new Pentecostals gather—have sprung up everywhere. They are usually ecumenical. That is, they draw people together from several denominations. Churchmen who have given their lives to bringing Christians together, with mixed success, look on this in amazement. Almost overnight, one of the most successful ecumenical endeavors springs up, and no Council of Churches organized it. Truly remarkable. The largest sales in the religious book field are books describing the Pentecostal experience. Christians who have dragged themselves to church over the years now tell everyone that church, prayer, Bible study, and salvation finally mean something real to them—and their praise goes to the Holy Spirit. At one point, nearly every Lutheran minister in Montana spoke in tongues, and the staff at the Episcopal headquarters in that state has a period of tongue speaking on their daily agenda. Over twenty thousand Roman Catholics—lay and religious alike—gathered at Notre Dame for a Charismatic Conference. And this is but one of many such conferences around the country, all of which draw enormous crowds.

It is clear from these few facts that the Pentecostal explosion has an unusual character for a religious happening. It is a movement within established churches. That is, a Lutheran or a Catholic adopts the practice of the gifts of the Spirit, but he remains within his own church. Even though there are plenty of Pentecostal denominations around to join, these people insist that the Pentecostal experience belongs to all Christians. They claim that the spiritual gifts, long ignored by most established churches, mark the truly fulfilled Christian. If these Pentecostals had simply quit their own denominations and affiliated with a traditional Pentecostal group where such things were tolerated, the problem might have disappeared.

But many have chosen to remain within their main line congregations, a fact which has kindled intense controversy and dissension. In 1962, an Episcopalian rector of a large suburban California parish made the national news weeklies when he was kicked out by his vestry for both speaking in and encouraging tongues. A group of Southern Baptist officials got their walking papers for the same reason. The late Bishop James Pike told his congregations in northern

California that they should "have a psychiatrist present" if they insisted on dabbling in tongues. In hundreds of congregations throughout North America, congregations of nearly every denomination, pastors and people are squared off over this issue.

The Pat Boone family isn't the only casualty of the Pentecostal controversy in main line Christianity.

But why is there such a sharp reaction to the movement, such a polarization of forces? Back of the reasons that are often cited, there appears to be one that is most basic.

There are two sharply different views on how the Spirit manifests himself. In general, denominations have opted for what we might call the continuing-collective approach, for reasons we will get to later. This point of view says that the church, viewed as an institution with a teaching authority, is the true vehicle for God's Spirit. When asked about his stand on Pentecostalism, Dr. Robert Marshall, president of the three million member Lutheran Church in America, snapped back: "I still believe the Holy Spirit works his miracles through the church." In other words, God's Spirit somehow or other works through the structures of the church.

The other stance could be called the individual-spontaneous view. Individuals can have direct contact with the Spirit. The gifts of the Spirit come directly to persons, apart from the sacraments or authority of the church structure. One's relationship with God becomes very personal and individual. Each individual knows he is right with God not because a church tells him so, but because he has personally experienced, at some emotional level, an assurance that this is so.

This controversy is as old as Christianity itself. The continuing-collective view of the Spirit's work has dominated in history, but it has been challenged now and then by the individual-spontaneous view. Supporters of the former have claimed that an individualized approach would fragment Christianity beyond repair, as each Christian went about believing and doing his own thing. Who is going to decide whether or not it is really the Spirit speaking to a man, or his own subconscious mind? Churchmen claim that the authority to make this distinction rests, in the final analysis, with the church as a collective, structured organization—whether this authority rests in a pope's pronouncement or in the consensus of elected delegates to a convention.

Supporters of the individual-spontaneous view assert that over the years these big ecclesiastical establishments have become more concerned with institutional survival than with God's Spirit. They are cold and dead. They engage in programs and activities which have little, if anything, to do with the essence of the gospel, namely, the salvation of sinners.

Back of these two approaches to the Spirit, there are two ways of reading and understanding what the Bible says about the Spirit. Both the Pentecostals and the non-Pentecostals accord the Bible a special authority. But they disagree sharply when they interpret what the Bible teaches. Therefore, a good way to begin to unravel this controversy is by looking at the divergent ways in which they understand the biblical witness.

CHAPTER TWO

WHERE IT ALL BEGAN

When Pentecostals turn to the Bible, they find hundreds of references to the Spirit. What they often overlook is that the term "Spirit" has different shades of meaning in the Bible. After all, the book was written over a period of perhaps ten centuries. Some development of ideas is expected. Differences between the Old and New Testament uses of the term should not surprise us, nor should differences within the New Testament between writing referring to Jesus' days on earth (the Gospels) and writings after Jesus' resurrection (the Acts and the Epistles).

For instance, the Spirit is spoken of in both Testaments in two different ways. One describes his working as a continual presence of God, a continuing power in the midst of human life to enable man to do God's will. This view, going back to the time of the great prophets, could be called the "continuing-collective" approach to the Spirit. Regular churches would prefer citing these passages as examples of the Spirit's mode of operation.

But there is also a second way of expressing the Spirit's activity, one more in keeping with the "individual-spontaneous" view. These passages talk of the Spirit as giving special power to certain individuals in specific situations. In the Old Testament they generally tend to be earlier than the other view of the Spirit.

A brief look at some specific references to the Spirit in the Bible may help show how both views of the Spirit, one charismatic and the other less dramatic, run together.

Where It All Began

The word used for the Spirit in the Hebrew of the Old Testament is the same word used for "breath" or "wind." When in the creation story of Gen. 2:7 we read, "The Lord God formed a man from the dust of the ground and breathed into his nostrils the breath of life," we can think of this as God giving his Spirit to man. This breath gave man life; thus the Spirit is a creative, life-giving force from God given to man.

This continuing-collective view of God's "breath" or Spirit was in the psalmist's mind when he wrote, "When thou takest away their breath, they fail . . . but when thou breathest into them, they recover; thou givest new life to the earth" (Ps. 104:29–30). The Spirit, in this sense, is the presence of God in life, an ongoing affair.

But there is another sense in which the Spirit is spoken of as a special gift, a charisma given to certain men. Elijah and Elisha, two early prophets whose stories are filled with what we would call magical wonders, did their astonishing deeds by the Spirit of God. Such prophets held their office because of their special connection to the Spirit's power. The early judges of Israel, too, were charismatic persons. That is, they had special endowments to fill their role. As it is written of the judge Othniel, "The spirit of the Lord came upon him and he became judge over Israel" (Judg. 3:10).

As time passed, the gifts of the Spirit given to men were thought of in less magical and more ethical terms. They provided wisdom and goodness; the Spirit gave to men the qualities they needed to rise to a crisis. When the Israelites began to think about a coming deliverer (Messiah), they naturally viewed him as one especially endowed with the charismatic gifts of goodness and wisdom. Isaiah writes of such a future deliverer: "The spirit of the Lord shall rest upon him,/a spirit of wisdom and understanding,/a spirit of counsel and power,/a spirit of knowledge and the fear of the Lord" (Isa. 11:2).

But the work of the Spirit wasn't confined to bringing forth remarkable people. The average man had access to the Spirit every day. When the Spirit rested well upon him, he could go about his affairs with rich qualities of character that pleased God. In Isa. 61:1-3, we read a lovely passage describing such a person:

> The spirit of the Lord God is upon me
> because the Lord has anointed me;
> he has sent me to bring good news to the humble,
>   to bind up the broken hearted,
> to proclaim liberty to the captives . . .
> to proclaim a year of the Lord's favour . . .
> to give them garlands instead of ashes . . .

In Jesus' time, both of these ideas of the Spirit circulated. Every Jew knew he had access to the Spirit, through his religion, on a continuing basis without a special experience. He also believed that certain people might be chosen for a special measure of that Spirit.

Where It All Began

When Jesus began his public ministry, the Gospel account has him baptized by John the Baptist. On this occasion, the heavens open up and the Spirit descends on him like a dove (Matt. 3:16). This story obviously wants to connect Jesus with those in Jewish life who had special measures of the Spirit. The reference is back to Isa. 11:2, a prophecy of a coming deliverer.

But at the same time, Jesus himself is given to speak of the Spirit in the continuing, or ordinary, sense of God's abiding presence with us. In John 3:5–8, we read of Jesus talking to a learned seeker named Nicodemus. He tells Nicodemus that he must be born again, of water and the spirit, to be saved. "It is spirit that gives birth to spirit. . . . The wind [spirit] blows where it wills; you hear the sound of it, but you do not know where it comes from, or where it is going. So with everyone who is born from the spirit [wind]." Jesus apparently speaks of the mysterious presence of God. Being born of the spirit is, in fact, simply being born of God.

However, in Jesus' day, large numbers of people expected that God would soon intervene in human affairs in a dramatic way. He would set up his "kingdom" in the "last days." One sign of this would be increased activity of the Spirit, an outpouring of charismatic gifts which would raise up charismatic leaders. Perhaps they, like some Pentecostals today, weren't satisfied with the way the ongoing Spirit worked! It was too ordinary; the new age would be ushered in with truly extraordinary working of the Spirit. Jesus seems to have fed this notion himself. He often spoke of a coming Spirit, who would appear when he left (John 14). This is confusing at first. Did Jesus mean still another Spirit—besides the Spirit of God already around? Probably not. These references seem to refer to the expected outpouring of the Spirit which would mark the advent of God's kingdom. In other words, Jesus is promising a time in which the Spirit would work among men with greater force, energy, and transforming power.

That day when the Spirit broke loose is recorded in Acts 2. It happened on a Pentecost, or harvest festival, and was marked by truly unusual happenings. In one sense, this break out of wonders is a throwback to the time of the judges and early prophets, when the Spirit was known by the magic he performed rather than by the wisdom and graciousness he gave men. As we will see, the plethora of miraculous happenings attributed to the Spirit was short lived. Soon the more abiding qualities of his work gained the upper hand. The days of Jesus and those immediately following were in transition, as it were. From the perspective of the New Testament writers, the dramatic evidence of the Spirit's working served to assure believers that the New Age did indeed begin with Jesus.

The facts of the extraordinary occurrences of Pentecost are well known. Just before his ascension to heaven, Jesus told his faithful that they would be baptized by the promised Holy Spirit within a few days (Acts 1:5). So the remnant of the faithful returned to Jerusalem to wait. They spent their time in deep prayer.

It happened to be Pentecost, a Jewish harvest festival. The apostles were together in one place, when a sound like a "mighty wind" filled their house. Tongues "like flames of fire" rested upon each one of them. And they began to speak in other tongues as the Spirit gave them utterance.

They were speaking of the great things God had done, but as they spoke, they used languages foreign to them. Their hearers, from all parts of the world, were astounded that these men of Galilee could speak in so many languages. Others who listened said the band was drunk, even though it was only 9:00 A.M. and a bit early for serious

Where It All Began

drinking. If some hearers report an amazing multilingual event and others, a group of drunks, it seems that whatever actually happened was open to widely varied interpretations.

Peter wasn't a bit perplexed. He recognized this event as the promised outpouring of the Holy Spirit. He addressed the crowds, telling them that what they had just heard in tongues was what the ancient prophet Joel had predicted (Joel 2:28–32) would happen at the great final moment when God visited his people and ushered in a new age. Joel, like other prophets, gave people hope by promising a new day when Israel would be forgiven and restored to glory. That day, he said, would be accompanied by some remarkable signs and wonders: "Your sons and your daughters shall prophesy, your old men shall dream dreams, and your young men see visions"; in addition there would be some spectacular special effects involving the sun, sky, and moon.

As far as Peter was concerned, the Pentecost experience fulfilled this promise. If the events of Pentecost didn't fit Joel's script exactly, the preacher Peter contented himself with the main point: Joel talked about the new age to come and, with the Holy Spirit, the new age had come. Peter developed this text into a stirring sermon—the Bible does not tell us in what tongue he spoke—calling men to repent and believe in Jesus the Messiah. Some three thousand did, and the Christian church was born.

What can we make of this? Almost anything we wish, and we will find support from some learned thinker of the church. The word for tongue is *glossa* in Greek, and tongues are spoken of as *glossolalia*. The word usually meant "language, tongue"; but in the New Testament it has a technical meaning for a special kind of spiritual speaking under the Spirit's influence. The Acts story clearly states that at Pentecost, people of various places heard the apostles, who were Galileans, speak in their own languages. The obvious interpretation is that we are faced with a miracle of language, a wonder sign typical of those assumed to go with an outpouring of God. However, some hearers thought the apostles were drunk. This hardly suggests intelligible talk on their part, so the door is open to see this experience as a kind of enthusiastic, but somewhat irrational, babbling.

Also, the people who heard this speaking in "tongues" are listed by their countries, not their languages. Some authorities contend that foreign Jews could speak either Greek or Aramaic. The apostles all spoke Aramaic, at least in the Galilean dialect. That would mean, if true, that the entire Jerusalem crowd could understand the apostles without a multilingual miracle.

Immediately after the "tongues" episode, we read Peter's sermon. He told the onlookers that what they had just heard was a sign of the new age. But note well: Peter apparently could address the whole multitude in one language and be understood, at least by the three thousand who responded to his conversion appeal.

What conclusions can be drawn from the account in Acts 2? For one thing, it seems that the multilingual part was an obscure happening, interpreted differently by those who heard it. At the same time, the whole crowd could easily understand the language of Peter's sermon, which was probably Aramaic, the common tongue of Palestine. Some of the early church fathers claimed Pentecost was really a miracle of hearing, rather than speech. The apostles spoke in their own tongue, and the people miraculously heard them in their own languages.

A number of scholars claim that the Acts 2 account blends so many traditions current in the early church that

Where It All Began

it is well nigh hopeless to straighten them out. Pentecostals, needless to say, disagree vehemently. They read this event at its face value—at least as they understand it—and conclude that:

1. We have here the record of the baptism of the Holy Spirit, as Jesus promised.

2. The gift of tongues which accompanied it is a sign of that baptism.

3. While the apostles probably spoke in foreign tongues—as Pentecostals report happening frequently today—the key is that they spoke "as the Spirit gave them power of utterance." In other words, the Spirit announces his coming by endowing the individual with the gift of extraordinary speech.

4. The gist of this passage is not the power of tongues, for tongues are only a sign; the focus is the Holy Spirit.

With that last statement few scholars would disagree. Acts 2 is indeed the record of an extraordinary outpouring of the Spirit. But many scholars and pastors in the main line churches would argue against putting one-sided stress on this particular event. They would insist that other New Testament traditions about the coming of the Spirit, like the one embodied in John's Gospel, must also be taken into account. According to John, on the Sunday that he rose from the grave, Jesus appeared in a locked room where the disciples had gathered in fear. He bade them peace, and they were filled with joy at seeing him. Then Jesus repeated, "Peace be with you." He breathed on them—note the connection again between breath and Spirit—as he said, "Receive the Holy Spirit! If you forgive any man's sins, they stand forgiven; if you pronounce them unforgiven, unforgiven they remain" (John 20:19–25).

John places the reception of the Holy Spirit before Pentecost. Theologically, John connects the reception of the Holy Spirit with an experience of the resurrection, rather than making the coming of the Spirit a separate occurrence.

If the Fourth Gospel calls into question the validity of equating the Pentecost story in Acts 2 with *the* coming of the Holy Spirit, so do the last six verses in Acts 2. In verses 42–47 we have a summary of certain things the apostles did following Pentecost. These verses describe normal church life. The apostles shared the common life, broke bread, and prayed. They were drawn together in faith (even to the point of trying communal living). They daily attended the temple, and privately in homes broke bread (obviously a reference to some form of the Lord's Supper). Reading the story this way leads one to see the preceding Pentecost event as the account of the creation of the church. The church, as the Body of Christ, is here filled with God's own power. This might be what John had in mind when he associated forgiveness of sins with the Holy Spirit after Jesus' resurrection. The church has all the gifts of God; the Spirit lives in the church; he may be appropriated through the sacraments. Peter himself ended his sermon with the challenge, "Repent and be baptized, every one of you, in the name of Jesus the Messiah for the forgiveness of your sins; and you will receive the gift of the Holy Spirit." Thus, baptism gives the Spirit, and the soul is nourished by the Spirit through the sacramental fellowship of the church.

The priority of baptism over the coming of the Spirit here seems to support the view of the main line Christians. However, to complicate matters once more, there is another famous incident recorded in Acts 10 where the order stated by Peter in Acts 2:38 is reversed. This is the story of Cornelius; the event is sometimes called the "Gentile Pentecost." Cornelius is a military officer, a Gentile who

Where It All Began

apparently either joined the Jewish faith or else sympathized with it. According to Acts 10, an angel tells Cornelius that Peter is coming to visit him and give him further religious insight. In the meantime, Peter has his famous vision of all the creatures of the world living together. A loyal and rather exclusive Jew, Peter comes to realize the meaning of the vision: God has a place for the Gentiles in his plan. So, Peter visits Cornelius and tells him the good news of Jesus. Then the writer of Acts records, "Peter was still speaking when the Holy Spirit came upon all who were listening to the message. The believers who had come with Peter, men of Jewish birth, were astonished that the gift of the Holy Spirit should have been poured out even on Gentiles. For they could hear them speaking in tongues of ecstasy and acclaiming the greatness of God. Then Peter spoke: 'Is anyone prepared to withhold the water for baptism from these persons, who have received the Holy Spirit just as we did ourselves?' Then he ordered them baptized in the name of Jesus Christ" (Acts 10:44–48).

Contrary to his sermonic appeal as recorded in Acts 2, Peter here offers water baptism *after* Cornelius and his household manifested the Spirit through tongues. The term translated "tongues of ecstasy" is the same word used in Acts 2: *glossolalia*. The translators made the judgment that the tongues spoken in this case were not foreign languages, but rather unintelligible sounds expressing intense delight and joy.

Thus, the tradition on the relationship between baptism and the Spirit embodied in the Cornelius story partly contradicts the earlier Pentecost story. In both accounts there is emphasis on the great wonders of the Spirit which accompany the proclamation of the gospel. This theme runs through the whole Book of Acts. But on the problem of the relationship of the Spirit to water baptism, Acts is less clear and unified. Most Christians who try to understand the Bible historically would say that the disagreements in Acts reflect the uncertainty of the early church on this matter. When Acts was composed, sometime before the end of the first century, the relationship between the coming of the Spirit and water baptism had not yet been clearly defined.

In Acts 19, we read of Paul coming to Ephesus, where he found a small band of converts. They had been disciples of John the Baptist, and were baptized by him for repentance. Paul offers them baptism in the name of Jesus (19:4) and they accept. And "when Paul had laid his hands on them, the Holy Spirit came upon them and they spoke in tongues of ecstasy and prophesied" (19:6). What divides Christians here is the question of whether or not receiving the Spirit is a definite event subsequent to receiving Christ, either through baptism or a faith conversion. Pentecostals believe it is, while most other Christians declare the two are somehow or other mixed together.

Besides these passages, Pentecostals point out the Samaritan revival under Phillip's preaching (Acts 8:4–17) and Paul's own extraordinary conversion experience (Acts 9:1–11) as two more major events in the earliest church in which receiving the Holy Spirit can be distinguished in time from receiving Christ.

This discussion shows us that both main line Christians and Pentecostals can find proof texts to bolster their arguments in the Book of Acts. Insofar as one sticks with the narrative in the Book of Acts, the Pentecostals have this edge: the earliest church felt there was such a thing as a definite experience of the Holy Spirit, and the coming of the Spirit was accompanied by signs and wonders of various kinds.

Where It All Began

Main line critics of the Pentecostals, on the other hand, would insist first that the Pentecostals rely too exclusively on certain passages in the Book of Acts. We aren't at all sure how Acts was put together. What are Luke's sources? What is his purpose in writing? Since he obviously does not tell all, what criteria does he use in selecting events? Those who do not accept the word-for-word literal authority of the text we have—and these are probably the majority of Christians—feel that without answers to questions like these, we cannot base doctrines on the Book of Acts, unless they are heavily buttressed in other New Testament writings. As we have said, there are quite probably several "doctrinal traditions" embodied in Acts. After all, an expanding movement didn't have time to formulate the faith into the kind of neat doctrinal statements we are used to. All we know for sure is that Acts gives big play to the work of the Spirit in various ways.

Second, we have a tradition which began quite soon in the postapostolic church. According to this tradition the wonderful events recorded in Acts were special gifts of God, given for that period and that period alone. It isn't hard to imagine how this idea came about. By the second century, folks noticed that the business of Christianity was being conducted in a much less spectacular manner. Two explanations were possible: either the church had hit the skids or Acts was a fairy tale. Neither of these explanations appealed to the theologians of that time, so they took a middle course. The events in Acts are true enough, they argued, but they were extraordinary happenings by which God got his church off the ground. We cannot expect them to continue.

A third argument of main line critics of Pentecostalism is again a biblical argument. This time the reference is to Paul's First Epistle to the Corinthians, chapters 12–14, in which the apostle refers to abuses of the kinds of gifts spoken of in Acts.

The Corinthians' congregation was made up of Christians living in a licentious seaport town called Corinth. The gifted Corinthians did everything a little too well. Apparently they had some real instincts for religion, but their excesses and extremes so distorted Christianity that Paul shed tears of anger and frustration over them. They had spiritual signs in abundance, yet they were falling apart as a community. So Paul tries to give them fervent and sound advice about keeping a perspective on things. The key section for our consideration is 1 Corinthians 12–14, a section which Paul begins simply, "About gifts of the Spirit, there are some things of which I do not wish you to remain ignorant."

These three chapters are well worth reading through, to get a clear impression of Paul's view of the total picture. The reader is first struck by the fact that Paul does indeed accept and assume spiritual gifts of a remarkable kind. He recognizes without hesitation that the whole Christian community is bound together by the Spirit. Even one's faith in Christ is a gift of the Spirit. The Spirit in fact offers a variety of gifts, which he lists: being able to declare that Jesus is Lord; wise speech; putting deep knowledge into words; faith; healing; miraculous powers; prophecy; distinguishing true from false spirits; ecstatic utterances of different kinds (tongues); the ability to interpret these utterances.

Each of these has its place, according to Paul. He uses the image of the body, made up of many parts, to illustrate how these gifts working in harmony can benefit the whole community. But his chief aim is to establish a true brotherhood, a real community of concern and love, a corporate body which expresses the Spirit in all of its relationships.

Where It All Began

In each of us the same Spirit is manifested in diverse ways "for some useful purpose" (12:7). When the gifts cease being "useful," upbuilding community and love, they are wrong. He has a hierarchy of gifts and tells the Corinthians, "The higher gifts are those you should aim at" (12:31). What is the highest gift? Paul says, "And now I will show you the best way of all" and goes on to his famous hymn to love, 1 Corinthians 13: "If I speak with the tongues of men or of angels, but if I am without love, I am a sounding gong or a clanging cymbal. . . ." He concludes his magnificent passage by saying that tongues of ecstasy, like knowledge and prophecy, will one day cease. "There are three things that last forever: faith, hope, and love; but the greatest of them all is love."

He then goes on: "Put love first; but there are other gifts of the Spirit at which you should aim also, and above all prophecy" (14:1). While the liberal strain in Christendom delights in the thirteenth chapter, it ignores the start of the fourteenth. Paul glorifies love, but he obstinately affirms the reality of other gifts, something many of his modern followers hesitate to do for fear of being too supernatural. However, Paul elevates the gift of prophecy over tongues.

"When a man is using the language of ecstasy [tongues] he is talking with God, not with men, for no man understands him; he is no doubt inspired, but he speaks mysteries. On the other hand, when a man prophesies, he is talking to men, and his words have power to build; they stimulate and they encourage. The language of ecstasy is good for the speaker himself, but it is prophecy that builds up a Christian community. I should be pleased for you all to use the tongues of ecstasy, but better pleased for you to prophesy. The prophet is worth more than the man of ecstatic speech—unless indeed he can explain its meaning, and so help to build up the community" (1 Cor. 14:2–5). Paul admits he prays in tongues himself, but adds "in the congregation I would rather speak five intelligible words, for the benefit of others as well as myself, than thousands of words in the language of ecstasy" (14:19). He ends with some practical directions. They should let no more than two or three speak, one at a time, in tongues, and someone should be around to interpret. Emphasize preaching. Do things decently and in order.

There is no denying that many primitive Christians, including Paul himself, spoke in tongues. But as early as this letter by Paul we have a strong caution to look beyond this one gift to the larger picture. The Spirit gives many gifts; tongues, frankly, are one of the lesser. Press on toward love and community. For this, preaching is going to help more than tongues.

Paul's note of caution about spiritual gifts, in which he puts down the "wondrous" elements and stresses the higher, ethical elements, fits in well with what he wrote some years earlier to the congregation in Galatia: "But the harvest of the Spirit is love, joy, peace, patience, kindness, goodness, fidelity, gentleness, and self-control. . . . If the Spirit is the source of our life, let the Spirit also direct our course" (Gal. 5:22, 25).

It seems that in less than a generation, the New Testament church had gone the full circle about the Spirit which the Israelites traveled: from a focus on his wonders to a stress on his power for godly living.

The church as a whole followed the lead of St. Paul. It adopted the view we have called the continuing-collective view of the Spirit. Asserting that the Spirit is an ever-present reality in the believer's life, it claimed that he could be received through the sacramental life of the church—such as baptism and worship.

Where It All Began

Why then do the Pentecostals interpret the biblical evidence so differently? They do so, I think, because they *have* to—and that deserves some explanation.

If the church, holding to a continuing-collective view of the Spirit, becomes in a believer's mind dead, unwholesome, purposeless and seems to be moving away from God, that believer *has* to say that the church holds a wrong view of the Spirit. If he doesn't, he is saying that the Spirit of God makes believers lifeless, which is rather absurd.

The Pentecostal says, "OK, let's say the Spirit comes through the life of the church. Let's say he is manifested in godly living. Where is your godly living? Where is your joy? Where is your zeal, your closeness to Christ, your sense of peace with God?

"Now, I have discovered that a personal experience, an individual encounter with the Spirit—shown by my speaking in tongues and other gifts—does fill me with joy, zeal, and gentleness. In short, you get the harvest of the Spirit my way, not yours."

Pentecostals find the individual-spontaneous view *works* for them. And, since the New Testament teaching about the Spirit includes support for both views, they concentrate on the biblical texts which support their view—such as Acts—and ignore some others, such as portions of First Corinthians, which claim that tongues are a very minor gift in the long run.

Both sides can quote Scripture at length, but so can the Devil. Which side is *right?*

The question escapes a simple answer. The biblical evidence contains elements of both traditions—the continuing-collective and the individual-spontaneous—about the Spirit. The full doctrine of the Spirit developed later, after the last piece of the New Testament was penned. The church, for reasons we will look at in the next chapter, opted for the continuing-collective view. However, *if* this long-term, structured approach to the Spirit which most denominations espouse ends up by limiting the work of God's Spirit to a kind of reasonable growth with spiritual touches, it is wrong. That many Christians today feel the church is more dead than alive testifies to the limitations of the traditional approach. The Pentecostal protest against this "dead church" takes the form of a stress on the miraculous events associated with God's Spirit—especially the "gifts of the Spirit." Insofar as this protest calls the church to recover the power of God which belongs to it, it receives the endorsement of notable figures in the church establishment. Dr. Krister Stendahl, the dean of Harvard Divinity School and a leading theologian and biblical scholar, remarked that it would do the church a lot of good to be shaken up a bit by the Pentecostals. The final test as to who is "right" will be who best displays the "harvest of the Spirit" —those qualities of life St. Paul lists in Gal. 5:22. Anyone expressing these qualities in his life cannot be too far from the Spirit of God.

But this survey of the Bible has given some reasonably clear points which help our understanding of the Spirit, and which will help us evaluate any talk we hear about the Holy Spirit:

1. The idea of the Spirit develops within both the Old and New Testaments. It moves from wonder-working to a focus on supranatural power to fulfill the Father's will. The ideas associated with the concept of the Holy Spirit began with the early church (rather than Jesus) and were expressed in their doctrinal fullness *after* the New Testament was written.

2. In the New Testament, we find conflicting elements of tradition about the Spirit. The issue wasn't fully settled then. Strands of both the continuing-collective and indi-

vidual-spontaneous views are represented. Perhaps a full understanding of the Spirit involves a both/and instead of an either/or decision.

3. The Spirit is spoken of as God's force in the world, or God-with-us. He is a reality of the spiritual order, a transcendent and supranatural force—in short, God himself.

4. In both Testaments, the Spirit manifests himself in diverse ways. In the New Testament, which speaks of his "gifts," the chief emphasis is on gifts such as love and faith, rather than on gifts like tongues.

5. The Bible does not shy away from identifying the Spirit's presence with signs, wonders, and other miraculous events. While these are not stressed as ends in themselves, their presence must be recognized. The New Testament church, unlike much of today's church, fully expected God to do miracles. It, much more than we, was continually aware of living in the presence of a power beyond its own —God's power.

A lot of church leaders feel that the world has now outgrown this miracle filled, supranatural world view of the first century. Perhaps so. But the fact that thousands of "straight" Christians are flocking to the Pentecostal movement suggests that modern man may not be as secular and this-worldly as many suppose.

And that may be the clearest smoke signal from the tongues of fire.

CHAPTER THREE

THE FIRE DIES

The biblical evidence doesn't settle the Pentecostal issue squarely either way. This is the unhappy situation with many doctrines. They are implicit in Scripture, defenders can cite texts, yet huge numbers of believers, loyal to the Bible, remain unpersuaded. How can this be so?

Most doctrinal lines traced through Scripture can be interpreted in a number of ways. It also has internal inconsistencies, in some places. And many issues—which emerged later as doctrines—were still in the embryo stage when the New Testament, especially, was being written. Thus, the biblical materials record different traditions, current in the first century, about some issues. We cited, for example, the two traditions about the coming of the Holy Spirit: one in John 20, the other in Acts 2.

As time went on this plurality of teachings and traditions increasingly hampered the church's mission. Faced with conflict from the pagan world, the church could not let conflict rage unchecked within its own ranks. Issues on which the New Testament writers had differed could not remain unsettled forever. The church set out to establish the outlines of what it accepted as catholic, apostolic teaching. This body of teaching formed the basis for the collective-continuing view of the Spirit and of the church. This view prevailed precisely because the other alternative— the individual-spontaneous view, in which every man was entitled to form his own doctrines as "God gave him light" — would only have prolonged the agony of internal conflict.

The Fire Dies

How did the church reach its decisions? It made a collective judgment in this way: bishops, or leaders, of Christian communities in various cities or towns very early assumed teaching authority in their own jurisdictions. When the bishops differed, it didn't matter too much at the very beginning. But soon, as the church felt it was a "world church" and not "the church in Rome" or "the church in Antioch," some semblance of agreement became essential. Bishops would come together to seek agreement —by vote if necessary. By 325, this process was formalized into what became a series of ecumenical councils. These councils eventually gave the church its basic creeds.

Scripture was the basic norm for these councils, but Scripture had to be interpreted. Basically those interpretations survived which had the allegiance of most Christian communities. Certainly we can find more than a few traces of politics, some of it rather brutal; and the big cities, such as Rome, carried more weight than representatives of lesser towns. But, broadly speaking, the decisions simply made official what was already "mainstream" thinking.

In this process, the matter of the Holy Spirit was settled. Though his role in the divine economy was never spelled out as thoroughly as were the person and work of Jesus, two significant points were established as official doctrine:

1. The Holy Spirit was said to work in and through the church and its sacraments. The Holy Spirit in fact was thought to guide the church in its process of establishing official catholic doctrine. This meant, in effect, that any individual experience of the Holy Spirit which led one counter to the discipline, authority, or teaching of the church was a false experience.

2. The Holy Spirit was established as one of the persons of the Godhead, in what has been called the Holy Trinity. This is a complex doctrine, covering the relation-

ship of the Father, Son, and Holy Spirit. One God, three persons. In modern terms, we might say one person (God) manifest in three personalities (Father, Son, Holy Spirit). But for our purposes, the main point is that the Holy Spirit was declared coequal with God.

It is interesting and worthwhile to trace this development of catholic orthodoxy during the first centuries, for it was mainly in reaction to those who stressed "spiritual gifts" and the individual-spontaneous conception of the Spirit that the church's continuing-collective doctrine of the Spirit took definite shape.

Three of the earliest nonbiblical, Christian writings that have survived are the *Didache, The Shepherd of Hermas,* and the *First Epistle of Clement to the Corinthians.* They were written about the same time as some of the later New Testament writings (ca. A.D. 100), and their references to the Spirit's activity are quite similar to those found in the Book of Acts. They speak of prophecy in the Spirit. This is different from tongues. Prophecy, as a charismatic gift rather than a deliberately wrought sermon, is a message offered by an individual in his normal tongue which contains a message from God. In modern Pentecostal circles, these messages are normally couched in the first person, indicating God himself (or more usually, Jesus) is speaking through the human vehicle. We can assume that prophecy in the early church resembled this. Clement speaks of a "full outpouring of the Holy Spirit" coming upon the Corinthians, but such language may or may not refer to charismatic signs. When he says that people spoke by the grace of God, he may mean nothing more dramatic and spectacular than what we mean when we say, "I finally —by the grace of God!—made it through my speech."

Ignatius, a second-century bishop, refers tantalizingly to a gift he must use with restraint and humility; we don't know exactly what it was, but we do know Ignatius was prone to seeing visions. A reference in an ancient document, called the *Martyrdom of Polycarp,* has this venerable bishop praying before his death for a full two hours "full of the grace of God," so that the people were astonished. This points to a spiritual event, but one with which noncharismatic Christians are familiar. None of these references really makes a case for special spiritual gifts.

But another second-century father, Irenaeus (ca. 125–202), who wrote one of the first summations of the Christian faith, which he entitled *Against Heresies*, speaks of tongues and other charismatic gifts in this work as if they occurred quite regularly among Christians:

> For some do certainly and truly drive out devils, so that those who have been cleansed from evil spirits frequently both believe, and join themselves to the Church. Others have foreknowledge of things to come; they see visions, and utter prophetic expressions. Others still, heal the sick by laying their hands upon them. . . . Yea, moreover, as I have said, the dead even have been raised up and remained among us for many years. . . . In like manner we do also hear many brethren in the Church, who possess prophetic gifts, and who through the Spirit speak all kinds of languages, and bring to light for the general benefit the hidden things of men, and declare the mysteries of God. . . .[1]

[1] Alexander Roberts and James Donaldson, *The Ante-Nicene Fathers* (Grand Rapids: Wm. Eerdmans Company, 1950–51), quoted by Morton Kelsey, *Tongue Speaking* (Garden City: Doubleday and Company, Inc., 1964), pp. 35–36.

Justin Martyr (ca. 100–165) developed the theory that the Spirit had come with Christ, then ceased, only to return after a while, giving special gifts to believers he finds worthy. "Now it is possible to see amongst us women and men who possess gifts of the Spirit of God. . . ." This reference neither defends nor denies tongues or any other specific gift. We can only assume, for we do not know, that Justin had in mind the same list of gifts Paul compiled in First Corinthians. But it is interesting that he needed a theory to explain the absence of gifts for a period of time.

So far, it seems that by the middle of the second century, the spiritual gifts spoken of in Acts and First Corinthians have begun to disappear. They occur more in some regions than in others, but they are no longer the normal way for a Christian to manifest the Holy Spirit.

One man, about this time, must have felt that the lack of visible gifts proved the church had lost the true Spirit. His name was Montanus, a Christian from Phrygia. In his heyday, he commanded an enormous following.

Though it seems odd, Montanus styled himself as a church reformer. We don't often think of the early church needing reformation, but Montanus did. Disgusted by the lackadaisical attitude of Christians toward pure living, incensed by the willingness of many bishops to reinstate those Christians who forsook their faith during persecutions, Montanus set about to purify the church.

He firmly believed that the Holy Spirit dwelt in him, using him as God's instrument. Needless to say, he wasn't about to submit to the authority of the established bishops. His followers believed that the gifts of the Spirit, especially prophecy and tongues, were restored to the church through his ministry. He taught an austere life, through which one prepared for the immediate return of the Lord. Eventually, his puritanical morality degenerated into legalism and his noble enthusiasm turned into sour arrogance. His movement was declared heretical. By about 220, it had died out. With the end of Montanism, we have the close of the first "Pentecostal renewal."

Why was his movement stopped? Because Montanus displayed the charismatic gifts? Not entirely; these gifts still showed up here and there without causing panic among bishops. The issue with Montanus ran much deeper—into channels which we can see today.

Montanus was an "enthusiast" who felt he had a special revelation which lifted him above the common herd. The bishops, as we noted, sensed that the survival of the church in troubled times depended on some sort of central teaching authority. The solidifying Christian tradition—later called the orthodox faith—had no room for private "Spirit-filled" ideas. The Spirit of God was public property, accessible to all Christians through the church and its sacraments.

There is a parallel between the Montanists and modern Pentecostals. Like the Montanists, modern Pentecostals talk of spiritual gifts in a different way than the established churches. From the standpoint of these churches, they have what amounts to a "private" idea, in contrast to a "public" faith. The first Pentecostals in our century ended up forming their own denominations, because they violated the public, accepted teaching of their former denominations. The newer Pentecostals, sensing their perilous situation in terms of their own denominational doctrine, often work frantically to put their best foot forward. That is, they strive to show how their use of spiritual gifts is really a fuller expression of what their churches already teach about the Holy Spirit, and not a "new" or "private" idea of their own.

Tertullian, the first Latin father, flourished around 200.

He was deeply influenced by the Montanist movement, perhaps more so by its severe asceticism than by its charismatic emphasis. In one writing he attacked the heretic Marcion. Tertullian demanded that Marcion prove his authentic Christianity by displaying some visions, prophetic gifts, rapturous speech, and interpretation of tongues. Tertullian claimed such evidential signs were abundant on his side, as they surely were among Montanists. However, Tertullian stressed rapture and ecstasy, that is, visionary trances and uncontrolled utterances. Modern Pentecostal phenomena such as tongues are not rapturous; one does not leave his senses in any visible way. Tertullian may have been referring to the sort of excessive subjective spirituality which brought about the eventual condemnation of the Montanists by the church.

Origen (185?–254?) was a church father who worked in Alexandria. Apparently he knew nothing about contemporary tongue speaking. In his famous apologetic work *Contra Celsus,* he denied that Christians ever uttered such prophecies. But Celsus was a pagan, and Origen was attempting to persuade him, so he might have twisted the facts to save embarrassment. In any case, Origen likely wouldn't have cared about such gifts. He worked in Alexandria, the cultural-university think tank of his day. His love affair with things philosophical and his reasonable bent of mind led him away from enthusiastic phenomena. He seems to have interpreted 1 Cor. 14:18 as referring to conscious, intelligible speech on Paul's part.

About 346, an obscure Egyptian abbot, St. Pachomius, is said to have spoken in the "language of angels." This probable reference to tongues is the last mention for nearly ten centuries. With the final passing of Montanism, we may assume charismatic gifts went out of style.

Chrysostom, one of the greatest church fathers, bishop

of Constantinople and the patriarch of Eastern Christianity, wrote in the fourth century that he doubted if men could speak in ecstasy anything they could not say rationally. With reference to 1 Corinthians 12 and 14, he frankly states: "The whole passage is very obscure, but the obscurity is produced by our ignorance of the facts referred to and by their cessation, for such things used to occur but now no longer take place."

Augustine, who flourished in the early fifth century, interpreted the story of Pentecost in Acts as a special miracle of God to assist the beginning of the church, but it "was done for a betokening and passed away." Later, when combatting the puritanical and enthusiastic Donatists, he wrote: "Who expects in these days that those on whom hands are laid that they may receive the Holy Spirit should forthwith begin to speak with tongues?"

Our sources for early church history are fragmentary and incomplete, but it is clear that the fires of the Spirit didn't burn very long with the brilliance of Pentecost. One reason may be that the church took the advice Paul gave to the Corinthians: it used tongues mainly as a vehicle for private praise and prayer. In that case, our historical records, which deal with larger and more public issues, would naturally ignore the phenomenon. And the early church, moving through a hostile Hellenistic world, tended to put its best face forward. The pagan Roman or Greek likely thought tongues were as weird as main line modern Christians think they are. If so, we can't expect the apologetic literature of this period to make a big thing of tongues, even if they were widely practiced.

The quality of these references to charismatic gifts is uneven; their conclusions and implications vary. The evidence, however, does seem to indicate that as time went on tongues and other charismatic manifestations fell into disfavor and faded away. But we can assume that, since different fathers wrote in different parts of the world, they reflected the situation in the area they knew best. Charismatic phenomena may always have flourished here and there in pockets, without becoming a general practice—with the possible exception of the period during the heyday of Montanism. The general trend, from all we can tell, moved definitely away from a general manifestation of charismatic gifts.

By the end of the period we are describing (that is, the period from ca. 100–500), the bishops were in firm control of the churches and were able to impose their continuing-collective view of the Spirit on them. If anything, the bishops' control of the church became even tighter as time went on, and the period of the Middle Ages (ca. 500–1500) shows little openness to the individual-spontaneous view of the Spirit. Augustine was a most important teacher of the medieval church, and it was his negative view of tongues that was generally accepted. Thus, when Thomas Aquinas compiled his *Summa Theologiae* (1267–73), he accepted the Augustinian position that tongues had been given for a particular purpose at a certain time—but that purpose had been fulfilled and that time was past. The Spirit now worked through sacramental and rational channels to effect his ends. The Western church had always had a rationalistic bent and Thomas was a great one for stressing the rational aspects of the Christian faith. St. Paul, he felt, always spoke "pure reason." Since Thomas thought that tongues and prophesying were irrational, he had absolutely no use for them. In fact, going even beyond Augustine and the early church, he equated the irrational with the demonic and suggested that such irrational "gifts" as tongues could only come from the demonic realm. Thomas's views soon became semiofficial doctrine. This

The Fire Dies

gave a new twist to the church's stand: charismatics were devil possessed! Insane! Or worse.

Now that the mark of the Devil had been put on tongue speaking there would be no more like St. Hildegard, a German abbess in the twelfth century who was known to speak in tongues. She was allegedly able to interpret Latin Scriptures, though she was uneducated, and could speak in unknown tongues. After St. Thomas became the theological norm, any sisters who followed St. Hildegard's path could expect trials as witches. The *Rituale Romanum* of the church provided orders for exorcism of those possessed by Satan, one sign of such possession being the ability to speak in a strange tongue or to interpret such a tongue when spoken. It is a fascinating, though morbid, speculation to contemplate how many tongue speakers went to their deaths as witches because of the Angelic Doctor's theology.

It is rather ironic that it was the irrationality of the charismatic gifts that distressed St. Thomas and the Western church. Most contemporary Christians who have received the gift of tongues insist that it is not irrational in the sense that it involves taking leave of the senses. One pioneer of the tongues movement in Lutheran circles, Larry Christenson, states bluntly that ecstasy is the wrong word to use in connection with tongues. "Those who *hear* a speaker in tongues are sometimes described as 'ecstatic' or 'amazed' (*existanto,* Acts 2:7; *exestesan,* Acts 10:45), but the speaker himself is *never* described in this way."[2] A number of Bible translations, such as the New English Bible, render *glossolalia* as "tongues of ecstasy," which Pentecostals call a mistranslation. They are quite sensitive about being thought of as possessed or out of their minds.

---

[2]Larry Christenson, *Speaking in Tongues* (Minneapolis: Dimension Books, 1968), p. 24.

Apparently, the early church worried about it too. Monsignor Ronald Knox writes: "But it seems quite clear that the orthodox of the second century, to whom prophecy was still a living though perhaps a rare gift, distinguished sharply between prophecy and alienation of the senses. St. Jerome, in explicit refutation of the Montanists, is forever assuring us that the Old Testament prophets had all their wits about them. This in spite of 2 Pet. 1:21, where we are told that saintly men, when they spoke were carried away by the Holy Spirit. In Montanus' time, and apparently in St. Jerome's, to be 'carried away in the spirit' was enough to bring a prophet under grave suspicion."[3] A passage in Tertullian makes this same point: the false prophet speaks in a trance, ending in a delirium over which he has no control.

In the East, the situation was a bit different. Eastern Orthodoxy broke with Roman Catholicism in the eleventh century. For some time previous to the break, the Eastern and Western traditions of the faith had taken separate paths. Eastern Christianity took on a more "pneumatic" or spiritual flavor. The West preferred reason, ultimately wedding Christian theology with the philosophy of Aristotle. The Eastern brethren felt that God gives many charismatic gifts. He offers a rich life of the Spirit. The Christian life is ultimately mystical, filled with wonders and mysteries. In this otherworldly environment, according to Morton Kelsey, perhaps the leading researcher into tongues, it is quite possible that *glossolalia* continued throughout the centuries. He finds Orthodox clergymen sympathetic to tongues, while feeling that such a stress on but one form of charisma suggests a poverty in the total spiritual life. No records exist of frequent tongue speaking

---

[3]Ronald Knox, *Enthusiasm* (Oxford: Clarendon Press, 1950), p. 35.

among the monks and other very devout persons in Orthodoxy, but scattered incidents have been reported.

Whether the major figures in the Reformation spoke in tongues or not is pure speculation. Luther, some say, had the kind of spiritual disposition which would lead to *glossolalia*, but there is no evidence that he ever spoke in tongues. Good, reasonable, austere Calvin seems an unlikely candidate for the charismatic gifts.

However, manifestations of tongues broke out among a small group of French Protestant Huguenots. This group remained behind after many of their brethren fled to the New World. Living in the Cevennes mountains, they were objects of intense persecution. A ten-year-old child, Isabeau Vincent, who could normally only speak in her own dialect, broke forth in an ecstatic experience with perfect, fluent French. Soon the Spirit seized the whole community. Reports describe children of three giving learned religious exhortations. Ignorant adults spoke in beautiful diction.

Priests claimed demon possession; the doctors who examined the children called it fanaticism. No one had an explanation, so they sent the children to the galleys, their death, or army service.

Eventually the movement went political under the title of Camisards. They were going to depose King Louis, as the Spirit had told them. They lost.

Also in France, a Catholic reform movement called Jansenism took the fancy of many learned men, including the great philosopher Pascal. Jansenites were much like the Montanists: a holiness sect with rigid morality. They would gather in a cemetery, around the grave of one of their more holy disciples, and speak publicly in tongues. Jansenism lasted about eighty years. It was eventually condemned by the church.

John Wesley, the founder of Methodism, loved religious

excitement. He and his fellow revivalists knew all about shaking and trembling and rocking and howling. But, as Monsignor Knox points out, in none of his journals does Wesley mention the gift of tongues. His stress on the Holy Spirit and sanctification took another turn. This is another instance which raises a flag of caution: we cannot associate reports of religious excitement, revivalism, and Holy Ghost talk with tongues or charismatic gifts. The two do not necessarily go together. Tongues can be a "cool" experience. (One Episcopalian business executive, who would no more pour out his sins crawling to the "mourners bench" than he would give up his American Express card, regularly speaks in tongues—in the most sedate, business-like manner possible!)

But if we cannot hear tongues in the noises of the Wesleyan revivals, we can hear the murmurs which will soon put the Pentecostal experience back into the picture. For that story, we must move on to the nineteenth century.

CHAPTER FOUR

THE FIRE FLARES ANEW

The period between the American-French revolutions and the First World War was one of the most turbulent and life-transforming periods in history. It began with an earth-shaking revolution in the doctrine of man. Freed from state and church, man established himself as an individual of dignity, with inalienable rights bestowed upon him by God himself. The stream of individualism flowed into the river of industrial expansion, creating an invincible flood of human progress which seemed ready to sweep the evils of poverty and degradation before it like dead trees. Those were good years to be alive—at least, for many people. For those left stranded by the sweeping river of prosperity, the American frontier with its springs of fresh water of new life beckoned.

Major social upheavals usually send shock waves into the stone sanctuaries of religion. The nineteenth century created a new environment for Christianity. In a way no learned doctor of the earlier church would have imagined, a strongly individualistic faith bored deeply into Protestantism. The spontaneous-individual view of the church challenged the collective-continuing view. Revivals, with their stress on *personal* salvation, became a religious movement of their own. Sinners shook before their stern Jehovah. Tears flowed as the caressing love of Jesus washed away sin's burdens in the stream of Calvary's blood. Freed from bondage to the state, the new man also felt himself emancipated from the grip of the church and its cultic life. He stood alone before God. The individual man on earth met Jesus, the individual man in heaven, and settled the matters of the soul.

As the century wore on, economic and technological progress leaped ahead. Machines doing the dirty work, locomotives moving a mile a minute, telegraphs sending messages over wires—it was hard not to believe that God's favorite creature was on the threshold of perfection.

This mood of infinite human progress infected religion, in the form of sanctification or holiness movements. Details varied, but in general these movements asserted that Christ not only freed a person from the guilt of his sins, but also freed him from the power of sin itself. The moral improvement possible for man seemed as limitless as his cultural and technological progress.

In the ferment of ideas, change, and renewal, the strange melodies of *glossolalia* broke forth. As we have seen, tongues were mostly silent after orthodoxy broke the back of the Montanist heresy. Why did they emerge in this century? Pentecostals attribute it to God's providence, his gift in the last days. Their critics figure that the smashing changes and social turmoils of the century hold the answer. Certainly a number of complex factors were involved.

Revivalism played its part. These mass meetings, which displayed a wondrous variety of religious enthusiasms, broke forth in the previous century, but in the nineteenth century they gathered real momentum. When science assaulted the sacred Writ, mighty defenders of God's eternal and verbal accuracy struck back from open platform, canvas tent, and gospel hall. Names of such great revivalists as Peter Cartwright, Charles Finney, and Dwight Moody are indelibly etched in the annals of American Christianity.

Revivalism contributed two things which later helped the Pentecostal movement explode in America: it made more people think of their personal faith in emotional

The Fire Flares Anew

terms, and it gave acceptance to lay-led religious movements. This last item broke the hold of the professionally trained clergy—who by education and inclination supported the "churchly" or collective-continuing view of the church. However, even though tongues and other gifts manifested themselves at some revivals, revivalism did not give birth directly to Pentecostalism. It served more as a midwife.

Besides these relatively infrequent appearances of charismatic gifts on the revival circuit, there were a number of other manifestations of spiritual gifts throughout the world. They apparently have no causal or geographic connection. They just happened, for some reason, in this century. They were certainly not part of an organized movement, for the "Pentecostal movement" as such did not exist in the nineteenth century. The number of these events and their seeming lack of connection convinces Pentecostals that God in his providence chose this period for an outpouring of his Spirit, perhaps because it was the beginning of the "last times." We can summarize but a few of these manifestations:

—In about 1830, tongues and healings appeared in Scotland. An invalid, Mary Campbell, one day felt suddenly strengthened and broke forth in tongues. In another city, a James McDonald, who also spoke in tongues, heard about Mary. He wrote her, commanding her to arise from her sickbed. She did, and lived a full, healthy life.

—In London, a prestigious Presbyterian preacher, Edward Irving, heard about the Campbell-McDonald incident and others. He became interested in tongues and other gifts. Though he did not speak in tongues himself (his big interest was predicting the exact date for the end of the world), he encouraged the gifts in his congregation. Soon his congregation became, in the words of one observer, a "bedlam" of tongue speaking and prophecy. Such staid parishioners as Peel and Coleridge became disgusted. Irving was eased out of his pulpit and died a young man in 1834. With his death, the huge outburst of tongues ceased, although some followers of his formed the Pentecostal-oriented Holy Catholic and Apostolic Church, which limped along as late as 1879.

—The Shakers, who settled in America, had a tradition of tongues going back to the prophets of Cevennes. In 1837, they enjoyed a ten-year revival marked by *glossolalia* and other gifts. Shakers also danced violently and lived in strange ways. Fortunately for them, the Salem witch trials had left a bitter taste in the public mouth. Otherwise, someone might have suggested proceeding against these "demonic" souls.

—The Latter Day Saints, America's most successful homegrown religion, incorporated belief in all spiritual gifts, including tongues. In their early days, hundreds of the saints of Salt Lake City spoke in tongues. They soon became the laughing stock of the "ungodly," so the leadership asked them to keep it quiet.

—In 1855, a great revival broke out in Russia. Tongue speaking appeared as one of several spiritual phenomena. It did not last for long, but it embraced—from all we can tell—vast numbers of people. A small group around the Black Sea continued speaking in tongues. These Armenians eventually organized as Pentecostal Christians and, as we shall see, had a monumental impact on the Pentecostal movement in the United States.

—The vision of Bernadette at Lourdes, in 1858, brought forth a rash of visions and prophecies, including many instances of speaking in other languages. Two German boys in 1869 are reported to have spoken in various classical languages. These incidents happened on Catholic soil, so they weren't received as coming from God. Tongues were

The Fire Flares Anew

signs of demon possession, according to *Rituale Romanum*. Therefore, priests exorcised the demons. Oddly enough, they had success in freeing the people from "possession." This leaves the ecclesiastical evidence on whether tongues are of God or of Satan somewhat cloudy. Much depended on whether the speaker lived in Catholic Europe or Protestant England and the United States. The records, for what they are worth, indicate that tongues can be exorcised, which is interesting.

—A Lutheran pastor by the name of Blumhardt is said to have conversed with demons, using foreign tongues. He was also involved in some exorcisms which took place at the well-known spa, Bad-Boll, during the 1860s and 70s.

—The pioneer psychologist William James reported seeing a young woman in the 1870s who spoke a tongue she could not understand, but which she was compelled to utter. The young woman was convinced it was a charismatic gift. James later wrote case studies on others with the same gift.

These scattered happenings would never have led to a movement of significance, except for another shift in religious thinking. Revivalists and others, following Wesley's line of reasoning, explored the idea of sanctification. Strictly speaking, sanctification is a religious word meaning "set apart for God." The revivalists were not satisfied, however, to speak of sanctification in general terms; they wanted tangible signs to help them distinguish the set-apart from the non-set-apart. One tangible way to show that one was set apart was to give up the sins and lusts of the flesh, such as alcohol, tobacco, saloons, painted women, cosmetics, bright clothing, and other appurtenances of wicked worldliness. Revivalists often went to great extremes in stressing this negative aspect of Christian life. (Yet one shouldn't dismiss these holiness disciplines too quickly. For all their excesses, they gave powerful impetus to the social reform movements which contributed so much to American life in the nineteenth and twentieth centuries. Such worthwhile groups as the Salvation Army sprang from the holiness movement, and they—not the established churches—moved with the gospel into the slums and saloons.) But the revivalists' search for holiness also led them down some more positive avenues. If Christians were to avoid certain vices, they were also to cultivate certain virtues or to seek certain gifts of the Spirit. Thus, the holiness movement sparked a renewed interest in the theology of the Holy Spirit. It did not directly support the notion of charismatic gifts—a few holiness people spoke in tongues, but most would not encourage it—but the movement did awaken interest in the workings of the Holy Spirit among believers. For later charismatics, this became foundational material for sorting out the meaning of their gifts.

By the end of the nineteenth century, we find a number of scattered groups rejoicing in tongues, increasing appearances of the phenomenon at revival meetings, a new interest in the long ignored Holy Spirit, and a general atmosphere which encouraged experimenting with new skins to hold the old wine. Religion had "come alive." A few "hallelujahs" were quite acceptable in Topeka, Kansas.

Which, as it happens, is where our story goes next. It is 1900, the end of one century and the beginning of a new. Secularist and religionist alike believed a whole new era of wonderful things was in the offing.

A former Methodist, Charles Parnham, was running a Bible school in Topeka. It was a small affair, operating from a converted house with about forty students. In December of 1900, he was out of town preaching and asked his students to study about the baptism of the Holy Spirit. They became convinced that speaking in tongues was the certain evidence of the baptism of the Holy Spirit.

The Fire Flares Anew

The students earnestly prayed for the Spirit. He came—on January 1, 1901. The proof? They received the gift of tongues!

Their experience made front page news in both Topeka and St. Louis, where they shared their experiences with the people at Bethel Bible College. They planned a big world tour, but it never came off. The whole idea just didn't catch on. Parnham then moved his school to Kansas City. In 1903 he enjoyed a little better success, with a string of meetings in Missouri and Kansas at which healings, tongues, and prophecy were reported. In 1905 he went to Orchard, Texas, where he converted the "whole town" (however many that would be, I do not know) and carried the revival on to Houston, where he eventually set up another Bible school.

Parnham would simply be one more little item to note in a summary list of isolated charismatic happenings, except for one thing: his preaching led directly to the event which gave birth to modern Pentecostalism. The birthplace is Los Angeles.

In 1906, a black woman named Neeley Terry came back to Los Angeles after a visit to Texas. Some of her friends there had received the baptism of the Spirit through Parnham's preaching. Intrigued, her church invited one William Seymour to come and preach. He arrived on an April Sunday. He preached from Acts, praising the gift of tongues, though he had not received the gift himself. He must not have gone over too well, for when he returned after lunch for the afternoon services, he found the deacons had locked the door on him. Having no place to go, Seymour found lodgings with one of the members.

After a couple of days, the people got to know Seymour better. Their attitude changed as they realized that one sermon doesn't make or break a pastor. They invited him to lead some prayer meetings.

He spoke about tongues. People asked him for the gift. He refused at first to lay his hands on anyone. But his host one night had a vision of the first Pentecost and he too wanted the experiences. On April 9, Seymour's host finally received the gift of the Holy Spirit. With Seymour, he went to another home where a prayer meeting of white people was in progress. The two entered, speaking fluently in tongues. As they came in, seven people were struck from their chairs at once and received the tongues.

Events this remarkable soon attract attention. For three days and nights, prayer went on in this house, which was usually packed to overflowing with seekers. Black and white Christians joined together to seek the Spirit. The streets soon jammed with people, all bursting forth wondrously in tongues. They found larger quarters in a former livery stable which had been converted into a church and then abandoned. They cleaned the place up and called it the Azuza Street Mission. For one thousand days, this stable was the fountainhead of Pentecostal waters, as the revival continued full force.

Small wonder that the little Azuza Street Mission holds a spot in a Pentecostal's affection as the birthplace of his movement. Jesus was born in a stable, so the shabby atmosphere has symbolic value. And the people who came to Azuza Street—both black and white, for the revival was fully integrated—went out to spread the news. Folks poured in from all over the country, pastors and laymen alike. Like a chain reaction, the Pentecostal experience multiplied in geometric proportions. Some twenty-six Pentecostal bodies—including the largest, the Assembly of God, and the Four Square Church, founded by colorful Aimee Semple McPherson—trace their beginnings to Azuza Street. Within fifty years, the original handful of 1906 had grown to over two million.

CHAPTER FIVE

THE FIRE SPREADS

The hot sparks from the fiery Azuza Street revival kindled an inferno in the religious world. It began as a bright campfire, but soon it spread to warm the religious establishment with a sirocco of lively enthusiasm.

Within fifty years, the small band in Los Angeles has drawn over two million in the United States—and about eighteen million more world wide—into a new and dynamic movement. Unnoticed from the tall steeples of organized religion, Pentecostalism burned deeply in the lower strata of society. The remarkable thing is how it moved up into the sanctuaries of the long-established, middle and upper middle class churches.

Those traditional Pentecostal denominations formed from the Azuza Street experience were hardly equipped to mount an assault on the citadels of established religion. For the most part, they were loose organizations—fiercely independent, thin on central organization, altogether more like loose federations than disciplined machines. The undisciplined atmosphere, with the ease by which nearly anyone could obtain preaching credentials, attracted more than a few outright frauds. Some Pentecostal preachers made Elmer Gantry shine like St. Francis by comparison. Jokes about the "Holy Roller" preacher rolling in the sack with his blond soprano became staples of ecclesiastical humor. They even allowed women preachers—which was at the time an "obvious travesty" on true religion. But the Pentecostal movement—cradled in ignorance, raised in an outrageously permissive nursery, sowing its adolescent wild oats in scandalous behavior, and picking up twenty million adherents in the bargain—has now penetrated the inner sanctums of the establishment. How did this happen?

Oddly enough, the credit goes to two remarkable and outstanding individuals who, in different ways, bridged the gap between Pentecostalism and regular churches. But before we meet them, we need to know why they were heard. What had happened to make the established churches want to hear what these strange Pentecostals had to say?

While Pentecostalism was getting on its feet, the regular churches were faltering as the astounding crises of the twentieth century smashed their illusions of progress and the kingdom of God on earth.

In Europe, the disaster of World War I disillusioned Christians as much as it did nonbelievers. The optimism of the Social Gospel fell mortally wounded on the Fields of Flanders. No one wanted to listen anymore to bright-eyed appeals for "human progress by God's aid."

Theologian Karl Barth responded to this mood of despair. After World War I, he published his classic work, *A Commentary on Romans*. This book shifted the theological perspective upwards, for Barth was the first notable theologian in a long time to assert the ultimate priority of God over man. It was God's actions, he said, not man's, which would save the world.

Americans didn't suffer nearly so much in World War I, so the dreamy optimism of the Social Gospel held on a bit longer. But World War II brought Americans to the same place their European brethren reached years before. The great, peaceful, growing, healthy world spoken of by Churchill and Roosevelt never appeared. In its place stood an invincible Iron Curtain and the specter of atomic annihilation. The old optimism died, and many asked, "Where do we turn next?" American preachers began to read such men as Barth and Niebuhr, whom they once thought too pessimistic because they harped on human sin, divine redemption, and the primacy of God.

If the church was ready to think of a powerful, supernatural God once again, and if the Pentecostals were there with such a God who baptized with fire and the Spirit, how did the two get together? The gap was bridged by the two amazing individuals we mentioned before—Demos Shakarian, a layman, and Dr. David du Plessis, a noted Pentecostal clergyman. Each brought the Pentecostal message into established religion through different channels— Shakarian to the laymen and parish clergy, du Plessis to the highest levels of organized church life.

Demos Shakarian is an Armenian dairyman in California who comes from one of the oldest Pentecostal families. Demos's grandfather, then a child, was part of the pioneer Armenian Pentecostal movement mentioned earlier. He came to the United States when the Turks turned on the Christians, an event prophesied by an eleven-year-old boy in the village of Kara Kala. Demos's grandfather went to Los Angeles. One day, while walking down San Pedro Street, he heard the familiar sound of tongues which he knew in his homeland. He checked their source: the Azuza Street Mission! By a strange twist of history, the Armenian Pentecostal revival and the Azuza Street revival came together.

Demos grew up in the Pentecostal tradition. As a child, he suffered a hearing problem, which was cured by prayer. He wanted to do something significant for God in return. In 1938 he began holding street rallies. Later, he turned his business talent to organizing evangelistic rallies. By 1951, Demos was helping Oral Roberts put together his big crusade in Los Angeles.

But Demos Shakarian had a bigger vision. He nourished

the dream of a full gospel fellowship for businessmen, where laymen could share their Spirit experience. After a lot of difficulties, during which he drew heavily on reassuring prophecies from the Lord, Demos incorporated the Full Gospel Businessmen's Fellowship International (FGBMFI) in 1953.

The FGBMFI played an important role in bringing Pentecostalism from the storefront church into the Hilton Hotel. A good number of the first neo-Pentecostals in regular churches first turned on to the Spirit gifts in FGBMFI gatherings.

The FGBMFI sponsors retreats, breakfasts, conventions, and a number of other gatherings where the Pentecostal gifts are celebrated. It is a layman's organization with no pretensions of becoming a denomination. With about three hundred thousand members—and perhaps a total of one million who participate in some aspect of its work—the FGBMFI reaches significantly into many levels of society. Its magazine reaches over a quarter of a million subscribers and, in 1963, its national convention drew over one hundred thousand people to a large New York City hotel. The FGBMFI provides a respectable platform and focal point for all sorts of Christians who share the Holy Spirit experience. And their members actively spread the news to others.

While Demos Shakarian was influencing the main stream of Christianity through lay people and parish clergy, another leader, Dr. David du Plessis, was spreading the Pentecostal gospel in more rarified circles. For his work, he is justly labeled "Mr. Pentecost."

A charming and gracious evangelist with a Scot brogue, du Plessis observed the changes that were taking place in the World Council of Churches after World War II. His interest was unique among Pentecostals. His charismatic

The Fire Spreads

colleagues thought the WCC was a step toward a World Super Church, which they contemptuously termed Satan's Whore. The Assemblies of God, in fact, often referred to the World Council as the "Scarlet Woman or Religious Babylon" mentioned scornfully in the Book of Revelation.

But du Plessis simply couldn't believe that God would let the Protestant world become Satan's instrument. He prayed about it and in 1951 received an answer: "The Lord spoke to me and clearly told me to go and witness to the leaders of the World Council of Churches." The fragmented Pentecostal movement would hardly tolerate an official spokesman in Babylon, no matter how much they respected du Plessis. So, he came entirely on his own, something of a gadfly.

Amazingly enough, the WCC leadership received him with remarkable favor. Regular churchmen were, by now, acutely aware that they were ossifying; they wanted to hear what this winsome and spiritually dynamic man had to say. In 1952, he addressed the International Missionary Conference of the WCC. WCC Secretary Visser't Hooft asked him to attend the Second Assembly in Evanston, where du Plessis spent hours in personal conversations with church leaders. These contacts led to further exposure: Princeton Seminary, Yale Divinity School, Union Theological Seminary, Colgate's Rochester School of Divinity, Southern Methodist University—the citadels of establishment theology. Those who heard him listened. Favorable comment about Pentecostalism and the Holy Spirit began to appear in regular church journals.

Du Plessis learned a lot, too. He found "a sincere recognition of the work of the Holy Spirit among the top echelons of Protestantism." He noted that tongues were "receiving more and more favorable attention." Du Plessis must have felt his mission to Babylon bore good fruit when, in a document calling for prayer, the WCC Commission on Faith and Order requested prayer for understanding the meaning of tongues. The document described the tongue speakers as people "who continually challenge and disturb the Church which all too easily becomes complacent and self-satisfied."

Meanwhile, Americans began to realize that Pentecostalism was strong in Europe. For example, one hundred thousand Swedes, usually assumed to be all Lutherans, belong to Pentecostal churches. One congregation alone, the Filadelphia Church in Stockholm, counts six thousand five hundred members. That's a respectful percentage of the church-going Swedes.

And neither European nor American realized how rapidly the Pentecostal movement was moving throughout the Third World. Rising nationalism in liberated colonies made it hard for foreign missionaries to remain, but Pentecostalism encourages lay leadership, and lay workers provide the ideal vehicle for indigenous evangelism. In Africa, Pentecostal evangelist Nicholas Bhengu—the Zulu son of a Lutheran pastor, and speaker of six languages besides tongues—would sometimes baptize one thousand three hundred converts at a clip.

Latin America proved fertile soil for the Spirit movement. The Methodist Pentecostal Church of Chile has seven hundred fifty thousand members. The Brazilian Assemblies of God number over one million two hundred thousand. While the Catholic church and regular Protestants floundered on this continent, the Pentecostals were growing faster than they could count. It reached the point where non-Pentecostal missionaries to twenty-two Latin American countries begged Dr. du Plessis to give them his "technique." He did: "Baptism into the Holy Spirit, by the Lord Jesus Christ, the mighty Baptizer."

The Fire Spreads 53

With so much going for them around the world, some kind of international Pentecostal organization was inevitable. The first World Pentecostal Conference was called in 1947. Few expected a big turn out; after all, Pentecostals suspected organization. But a remarkable three thousand did show up for the Zurich meeting. Over the years, Pentecostal pride in the World Conference grew. By the time of the Eighth World Pentecostal Conference, held in Rio de Janeiro, some one hundred twenty thousand delegates attended.

Dr. du Plessis, in a wise move, was elected secretary of the WPC. The delegates also established a journal of international Pentecostalism, called *Pentecost*. Under the able editorship of Donald Gee, an Englishman, this magazine soon gained wide respect in all church circles.

And of course the Roman Catholic church, in the Vatican II renewal under Pope John, became very interested in the same spiritual renewal that had gripped the WCC leadership. Protestant and Catholic alike developed an intense new interest in the people with the gifts of the Spirit. The rapid expansion of the Pentecostal movement, and their huge World Conferences, caught the attention of the public media. The Spirit became news. And the ordinary straight Christian became aware, perhaps for the first time, that there might be something real and worthwhile in Pentecostalism.

The time was ripe for a reassessment of Pentecostalism and some experimenting with the Spirit and his gifts.

The year 1962 is a watershed in the history of Pentecostal growth, for this year showed the nation that Pentecostalism had spread to main line denominations. Dennis Bennett, an Episcopalian rector in Van Nuys, California, got into trouble over tongues, and found himself propelled into the national press. Morton Kelsey describes Father

Bennett's experience (*Tongue Speaking*, pp. 99–104), on which the following summary is based.

Father Bennett came to St. Mark's in 1953, when it was a struggling little parish. Under the dedicated leadership of this former Congregationalist who turned Episcopalian in a search for a richer sacramental life, the parish grew to a prosperous two thousand six hundred members, with a staff of four clergymen. Father Bennett accomplished this without the benefit of the baptism of the Holy Spirit, however. That came later.

A neighboring priest called him one day to report a strange happening. A couple who had been notoriously slack in their church attendance suddenly started coming to church regularly and displayed real enthusiasm for parish work. This priest was naturally curious about what wrought the transformation. He discovered that they and about a dozen others were meeting in some sort of study group. Father Bennett agreed to join him in checking this group out.

Father Bennett first met with the young couple who displayed this fresh zeal. They told him about the study group and for several weeks Father Bennett attended these sessions. The members of the group read the Bible and other literature on Spirit renewal, underlining and discussing significant passages. Other people, including some of Father Bennett's lay people, also became curious, so the group of seekers from St. Mark's expanded. Some of Father Bennett's fellow priests joined the crowd.

These meetings took place in private homes in the San Fernando Valley area of Los Angeles. In the area of Van Nuys, the housing tends toward three and four bedroom homes in the middle price bracket, catering to the typical suburban clientele. This is worth remembering, for "straight" Christians still have a prejudice that all Pentecostal happenings take place somewhere in a pile of sawdust. These people had the money, jobs, and future we all probably wished we had back in 1962.

As he attended these study groups, Father Bennett rather liked what he saw. Their openness to God impressed him. He inquired how he might receive tongues and was told, matter-of-factly, that it came "as a part of the package." The package was the baptism of the Holy Spirit. By this time, the priest wanted the gift badly. One night he and his friends prayed for one solid hour, but nothing happened. Somewhat chagrined, Father Bennett wondered if this gift were ordained for him.

Then, one Saturday afternoon, he broke through. During prayer with three others, he began to form words; not gibberish or baby talk, but words of some strange language. He stopped in a few minutes, feeling very tired. He sensed he had a strange experience, but he says he was not particularly moved or uplifted by it.

A few days later, he returned to the prayer group. A lay friend suggested he might be trying too hard. They retired to the den and sat down in comfortable chairs. Here they prayed and praised God. Soon the strange sounds of *glossolalia* emerged. He felt quite in control, so much so that if someone came in, he could ask them to sit down and then return immediately to his tongue speaking. Father Bennett says of that experience: "I realized what I was doing. It became clear, perfectly clear. I knew that God the Holy Spirit, whom I had never *directly* experienced in my life before, was putting these words on my lips. He was guiding, and I was letting him." He ran back to join the others in the living room shouting, "You mean that a Christian can feel like this?"

For Father Bennett, the good feeling did not go away. His new perception of spiritual reality empowered him in his ministry. He had, for instance, long practiced the dignified Episcopalian ritual of laying hands upon the sick. After his new experience, he noted that people now began to recover; the Holy Spirit had also blessed him with the gift of healing. The word of his remarkable encounter with the Holy Spirit spread throughout the parish. More and more people came to the experience of the Holy Spirit through groups he organized.

Why didn't all this lead to the ecclesiastical version of "and they lived happily ever after"? Here is a bright and aggressive minister, with two thousand six hundred people on his rolls, who gets really turned on to spiritual things, and who seems truly excited about his faith. What more could a parish want?

Apparently, much more, for Father Bennett was "kicked out" by his vestry. Since then the same story has been repeated again and again in the lives of other clergymen who speak in tongues.

We said that Father Bennett was kicked out. More accurately, he resigned in a power play. It seems that the tongues business split the congregation and the clerical staff. A good number of the folks weren't at all sure that they wanted the baptism of the Holy Spirit. Based on similar controversies with which I am familiar, I would guess that the matter of tongues was a side issue, although it may have been the most talked about. Tongues, as Father Bennett was told, come as part of a package. It is the package deal which so many church people reject. The package includes a new zeal, a strong tendency to make one's faith central in life, and an uncontrollable experience which makes it impossible to manage one's religious life in terms of what is most comfortable and convenient. Holy Spirit people get so excited they go around telling others to receive the gifts; like anyone with something to share, they ask you to come aboard. But while we tolerate the guy who tells us repeatedly, "You simply must get yourself a vacation home; it's the greatest thing for the family, we love ours, etc., etc.," we have far less tolerance for a person who insists we have to get the Holy Spirit, especially when we feel we are getting along pretty well with God. Many church members want religion that goes only so far, and some newly baptized Pentecostals have a tendency to go beyond that point. The predictable result is chaos and dissension.

Father Bennett thought he could ease the tensions by resigning. If the vestry refused his resignation, he would have a mandate to continue his ministry. However, the vestry received his resignation with a sigh of relief, leaving him without a call. Tongue speaking clergy in main line churches then—as now—aren't exactly in demand. Father Bennett finally landed a post in a tiny run-down center city church in Seattle. His superiors probably figured he could not do much damage there. As a matter of fact, he has the church growing dramatically, enlarging its program and busily turning on other priests to tongues—fourteen at the last count I have.

When Father Bennett resigned, the news was carried nationally and the media informed church people, perhaps for the first time, that something was happening in their midst. For that reason, 1962 is a good year to remember.

But Father Bennett was not the first non-Pentecostal minister to have this experience, though his story was the first to be nationally publicized. Pentecostal ministers have told me of fellow clergy from traditional denominations who, over the years, have come to them for the gift. Morton Kelsey in his book *Tongue Speaking*, to which we have already referred, tells the story of another Episcopal priest with a master's degree in theology who received the gift sometime in 1950–51. He had come into contact with the movement when his mother and brother received the gift of tongues and told him about it when he went home to Denver after graduating from the seminary. He went to a prayer meeting with them and had his initial experience with tongues, by repeating "Jesu, joy" over and over. Later, he had the full gift of tongues. He writes: "One of the more concrete results of this experience for me was the fact that the indwelling power of the Holy Spirit made me quite confident of my 'call' to the ministry." However, he later points out that he never really had any doubts about it anyway. For him, this experience was a seal and guarantee, a further assurance, that the path he had embarked upon already was proper for him. He has kept the gift secret, using it privately. There is no way to know the number of "underground Pentecostals," but I am prepared to accept a rather high estimate.

Though some tongue speakers feel that they must use their gifts privately, others are openly joining the neo-Pentecostal movement. One Pentecostal authority stated that by 1963, all but one Lutheran minister in the state of Montana had received the baptism; I can't verify the fact, but I did talk with a number of Lutherans who got turned on to tongues in that state. The Episcopal bishop in Montana is also keen on tongues, and Montana is a center of Episcopalian Pentecostalism. The staff of the diocese speaks in tongues regularly. I suppose someday we will be able to chart Pentecost's progress across the continent.

An experience at Yale in 1962 also attracted national attention. Some members of the Yale Christian Fellowship had contact with healing services and other renewal efforts, through some local churches. Others visited groups where tongues and prophecy were on the agenda. One member contacted the Reverend Harald Bredesen, a Reformed

The Fire Spreads

Church pastor who had received the gift of tongues, and asked him to speak to their group.

Pastor Bredesen met for prayer with a small group of students and with some of his own people in the president's room. Six students spoke in tongues. A faculty member peeked in to see what these odd goings on were all about, only to receive the gift himself a little later. This turned into a movement, in which a number of students received the Spirit, to the confusion of the three chaplains at Yale. The new Pentecostal students regularly held prayer services. Most said the experience wasn't particularly overwhelming, but it did make the Bible come alive and turned Jesus into a real and living person in their lives. As these students spread out to other schools and professions, they continued to report that the experience of the Holy Spirit enlarged their capacity to deal with daily life and tasks. Many were amazed to find that instead of a volcanic emotional experience or a psychotic freak-out, Spirit baptism amounted to a quiet source of identifiable strength.

Pastor Louis Evans had an outpouring of the Spirit in his parish (as reported in *Christian Life* 25 [July 1963]: 31). Son of the senior Louis Evans, who long shepherded the enormous and prestigious Hollywood Presbyterian Church and later became a sort of ambassador at large for his denomination, the younger Louis had the background and training necessary for skyrocketing success in his denomination. His first call was to form a church in Bel-Air, the most expensive residential area in Los Angeles.

Pastor Evans established a fine parish, with a fabulously expensive building on a mountain top, into which he shepherded his well-heeled congregation drawn from the movie colony.

Evans didn't need some new religious kick to keep him

from getting bored. Nevertheless, the baptism of the Spirit came, complete with tongues. He wrote of the experience: "This was disturbing at first, but the beneficial results it has brought to our people have overcome many objections we had. I have seen people desperately in need completely transformed as God the Holy Spirit demonstrated Himself to them through the ability to worship Him in another language."

The tongue movement flourishes at Hollywood Presbyterian Church as well. As major congregations and respected pastors in various denominations have this experience, which now happens more and more, the new Pentecostal outpouring will turn into a flood. Actually, some experienced Pentecostals have confided to me their fear that it will soon become the "in" thing to do, then disintegrate into a fad for want of proper theological understanding.

By way of helping people in various denominations interpret the gift of the Spirit in terms of their own traditions, the Full Gospel Businessmen's Fellowship International has prepared a series of booklets entitled "Methodists (Presbyterians, Lutherans, etc.) and the Baptism of the Holy Spirit." Pentecostals are convinced that since the baptism is the work of God, there must be a place for it in any Christian church. But many neo-Pentecostals have not been able to find a place in their own church, so they move into independent groups, such as the Holy Spirit fellowships which are springing up all over California.

If it strains the credulity to hear Pentecostalism has moved into main line Protestantism, it will stagger the mind to learn that the charismatic renewal has swept the Roman Catholic church. During the Second Vatican Council, Pope John prayed for a new Pentecost in his church. Little did he imagine how literally the prayer would be fulfilled. The deliberations of Vatican II unleashed a tornado of renewal efforts. Among other things, the venerable, if unintelligible, Latin Mass went out the door. In its place came another unintelligible tongue: *glossolalia*. There is no doubt that Vatican II created the mood and stance which enabled the Catholic Pentecostal movement to begin. By 1967, it was mushrooming.

Unlike its Protestant counterpart, the Catholic charismatic renewal began in universities, such as Duquesne and Notre Dame. Those who helped foster it were Roman Catholic theologians, many of them Mariologists. The numbers who attend the annual charismatic congress at Notre Dame chart the movement's growth. Beginning with a few hundred in the late sixties, by 1973 the conference drew twenty thousand. These conferences spawn Holy Spirit groups in local parishes. Priests and nuns attend these meetings, speaking with tongues, and testifying to healings. Prophecy also plays an important part among the Catholics, perhaps as much as tongues.

All this appalls some bishops, but the Catholics, who once considered *glossolalia* a sure sign of demon possession, have probably had less trouble with the movement than Protestants. Catholic theology, with its stress on the conveying of the Holy Spirit's gifts through the sacraments, provides a better theological basis for containing this movement within the church than most Protestant theologies. Speaking of the baptism of the Spirit as a second experience within a church that preaches one experience—Christ —and one only, causes troubles. But Catholics have always distinguished a time between the gift of adoption into Christ (baptism) and the later gift of the Holy Spirit (confirmation). Thus, Catholics tend to view their Pentecostal experience as one which simply gives fullness to their confirmation. This enables them to work within the sacramental framework of their church, which has long appreciated nonrational spiritual gifts of other kinds.

We don't have accurate statistics on the neo-Pentecostal movement. But if the Notre Dame conferences can draw twenty thousand, and various regional charismatic conferences, such as one held in Minneapolis which drew five thousand, pack them in, we can guess that the number of neo-Pentecostals runs between about six hundred thousand and one million. Traditional Pentecostals add up to two million. In a nation where sixty to eighty million go to church each Sunday, a total of three million Pentecostals may seem like a drop in the bucket. But while major denominations drop a few percentage points a year in their membership, the number joining the Pentecostal renewal increases explosively. Unless the whole Pentecostal business turns out to be a momentary fad (which doesn't seem likely), we can expect it to emerge as a significant issue in church life in the next decade, both in North America and Europe.

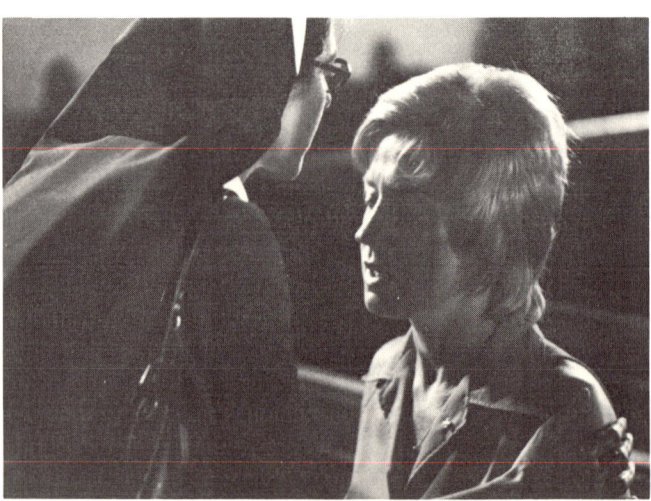

CHAPTER SIX

WHAT IS PENTECOSTALISM?

THE PENTECOSTAL EXPERIENCE

We already know a couple of things Pentecostalism is *not*. It is not a "new religion." We have seen that it has always appeared within Christianity. Nor is it a new "denomination," in the sense that Catholicism and Presbyterianism are self-contained, well-thought-out systems of doctrine. The traditional Pentecostal denominations borrowed their doctrine basically from existing groups. The neo-Pentecostals still hold their denominational allegiance. Pentecostal theology—their thinking about their position on the Spirit—almost seems to be an afterthought to their experience.

And that gives us a clue to the central thrust of Pentecostalism: it is an *experience*. Pentecostals who otherwise differ widely in doctrine and worship style unite in the bond of a common experience. That experience might be defined as an encounter with the Spirit of God in which the Spirit manifests himself by giving the believer certain gifts, especially the gift of tongues.

All Christians, of course, have had some kind of experience with the Holy Spirit. It is the type or quality of the experience which separates Pentecostals from straight Christians. The Pentecostals' insistence that their experience is the real and true experience of the Spirit—compared with which all others are mere shadows—raises a great deal of heat. Pentccostals right now don't seem able to accept a variety of equally valid experiences of the Spirit. For their part, straight Christians often react defensively, claiming the Pentecostal experience is a false and intolerable one.

Since both sides firmly believe in the Holy Spirit, differing only in their experience of him, they find they share a lot of the same religious language. But actually, each side uses the language in a slightly different way. Experience shapes attitudes. Our experience with religious life tends to mold the nuances of our religious language. In order to discover what Pentecostalism is all about, we not only have to examine the basic experience itself, but also look at the way this experience affects one's attitude toward other basic Christian positions.

We have discussed the experience itself. The story of Father Bennett is pretty typical of the way people receive the baptism of the Spirit. They sense an outside force—God's Spirit—entering their being. They speak in tongues and display other gifts. This describes the surface events, but what about the deeper meaning? What does this experience do for people? Why are they so enthusiastic about it?

First of all, Pentecostals from the main line churches uniformly told me that this experience made their faith more meaningful to them. Not only did Jesus become more "real," but quite often the practices of religion—worship and prayer, for example—took on richer qualities. Two quotes from the many new Pentecostals I spoke with express this very well.

A Roman Catholic: "I used to be careless about Mass. You know, if we had a late night or plans for a trip, I would either forget Mass or run off to an early one with my mind a million miles away. Now, after my baptism in the Spirit, I delight in the Mass and the sacraments and prayer and the whole business. I am a lifelong Catholic, with sixteen years of Catholic education. But for the first time, my faith really means something to me."

A Protestant: "I went to church pretty regularly, but I

don't think it meant much. For instance, I could never really pray. Spiritual things simply didn't matter in my daily life. When I received the Spirit, all of this became much more real to me. Jesus is now so personal to me, that he is like a friend or a next-door neighbor. I read the Bible and I actually enjoy it, something I never did before."

Somehow, through the kind of Spirit experience which leads to displaying the gifts, Pentecostals became stronger in the faith in certain ways. All Christian churches agree that the role of the Holy Spirit—God present in our midst —is to strengthen us in our faith, make it "real," as it were. Why these people found such effects only through the Pentecostal experience, and not through the normal life of the Christian church, is a matter we will look at later. We should point out that huge numbers of church people have found new and deep personal reality in their faith *without* the Pentecostal experience. These people could give testimonies very much like those we have quoted. But our interest is in why so many are finding this renewal of faith today through this particular form of encounter with the Holy Spirit.

The new Pentecostals find a second benefit from their experience. They sense a fresh degree of freedom in their faith, especially in their ability to praise God spontaneously. Tongues provide a vehicle, a language, for this praise. These people have learned to be as unashamedly delighted in what God does as they are when their favorite football team wins. Many non-Pentecostal congregations have lately tried to loosen up their worship services to provide room for spontaneous praise and freedom. Newer liturgies include modern idioms, guitar-led upbeat music, even handclapping. Many new Pentecostals are skeptical of such external changes and see the need for more profound changes. One put it succinctly: "Now I *want* to praise God;

it's in my heart, not my head." For regular Christians who only know the dignified and rather stuffy traditional services, the praise atmosphere of a Pentecostal fellowship can be literally intoxicating.

A third attraction of the Pentecostal experience is one more obvious to an outsider than to an adherent: the small group fellowship. Right now, the Pentecostal movement has a paradenominational character which makes it very attractive to certain people with certain needs. Small bands of "in group" people, those with the Spirit, gather either within the congregation or in ecumenical Spirit fellowships outside of it. Such small groups, as social scientists have known for years, provide a powerful support base. Encounter groups and other therapy groups—which are giving people essentially the same emotional content in a secular framework—all operate on a small group, intimate fellowship basis. When a mild sense of persecution enhances the quality of group life, through a sense of difference because each member is one of a select group, the feelings within the group become intense. Most Pentecostals call this feeling "love." One told me, "In this group, I can almost taste and touch love. People really care about me, and I care about them."

In a world obviously starved for love and emotionally-felt relationships, Spirit fellowship groups fulfill a deep need. Even the Pentecostal denominations are, in the larger picture of North American religion, much like small groups. The churches are independent, forming denominations on a "fellowship" or a federated basis among congregations, which jealously hang on to their individuality. Within congregations, people gather in small prayer meetings and study groups. The huge six thousand five hundred member Filadelfia Church in Stockholm holds one hundred fifty cottage meetings a week in private homes. Intuitively, the traditional Pentecostal churches have structured around the small spiritual fellowship group. The neo-Pentecostal groups have, often of necessity, followed the same pattern.

This tendency to cultivate small "in" groups makes the established church clergy mad. Pentecostals, they say, break up the church. This charge is partly true. The simple fact, however, is that large numbers of established denominational congregations do not provide any outlet for those members who wish to cultivate purely spiritual disciplines in an intimate fellowship group. Congregations proliferate groups around such goals as married couples enjoying a night out, or Boy Scouts, or supporting the parish. Some of the clergy, as a result of their theological education, cannot believe in Jesus in any fundamental sense as personal savior. Yet within their congregations are large numbers of people who respond to a concrete, emotional Christian experience and desire to explore those purely religious dimensions of life in which their pastors often feel terribly inadequate.

Critics, more than enthusiasts, would call the fourth item an attraction: the movement embodies a highly individualistic version of Christianity. It concentrates on prayer, inward spiritual growth, and personal blessings. It reaches out to the neighbor mainly in a spiritual sense, by witnessing for Jesus or offering testimony to the power of God's Spirit. Such intensely inward religious movements are nothing new; Pentecostalism in this sense is a direct heir of the pietist movements of the seventeenth, eighteenth, and nineteenth centuries. But pietism in any century often provokes anger because it is too inwardly individual to fit conveniently into the corporate structures of Christendom. And it usually has an ax to grind, for its very existence stands as testimony to the "coldness and sterility" of the established church.

Observers today note a more sinister tone to the trend toward inward and personal faith. The trend shows in such diverse forms as exotic Eastern meditation cults, pop-psych movements for self-development such as transactional analysis, the expressed distaste of churchgoers for their denominational curriculum and policies, the "back to the Bible" movement, and even the seven million plus sales of the avian epic, *Jonathan Livingston Seagull*. The trend is clear; its sinister side, say these observers, comes with the flight from corporate responsibility and a quest for justice, into the comforts of a personal faith. An exhausted population, it seems, turns from the horrors of the world about it to a crystal castle it creates in the never-never land of its own mind.

Is Pentecostalism a manifestation of this obvious trend? I ran across more than a little evidence that it is. One illustration will make the point.

A Presbyterian church in a Philadelphia suburb recently got caught up in the Pentecostal revival. It began when the pastor received the gift of tongues and Spirit baptism. He brought the charismatic revival to his congregation and—unlike some other instances which ended quite differently—his parishioners bought into it completely. Sunday morning they have the straight services, but in the evening they have praise services, where all sorts of gifts, including healings, break out. Their youth group bulges with enthusiastic, attractive youngsters anxious to convert their classmates, and new members pour in each month. It is enough to make an elder smile!

The enthusiasm in this parish impressed me. I wanted to know more. Since the real facts about a congregation come from the parish secretary, I spoke with this lady for awhile. She had served the church for twenty-five years, watching several ministers come and go. She told me the congrega-

What Is Pentecostalism?

tion loved what happened to their pastor. They could, she said, sense it almost at once in his preaching. How?, I queried. "Well, he always was a good preacher, in that he kept your interest. But he began to move away from all those social sermons and preached more and more from the Bible."

Could that move, and all it symbolizes, explain the "revival" at this church as readily as the host of charismatic gifts? I use this one congregation as an example, but many neo-Pentecostals in conversations indicated openly or inadvertently that one of the best things about their new religious life is that there isn't any of "that social ministry garbage."

The four attractions of Pentecostalism that we have listed are worth thinking about. They may not only tell us something about Pentecostalism, but they may also tell us something about the way the established churches have been doing their job. The fact that main line Christians are attracted to Pentecostalism may mean that their churches are failing to do their job properly; or it could mean that a lot of Christians want something the established church feels, in good conscience, it cannot give them. In the case of Pentecostalism, it is a little of both.

The first two attractions of the Spirit movement—its ability to deepen one's commitment to the Christian faith and to provide a place for adoration and praise—are undoubtedly legitimate attractions and point to failures in the established churches. The Pentecostal movement is filling an authentic vacuum here. The sacramental life of the church and the classic spiritual disciplines of the faith, if strongly cultivated, could provide for this dimension of Christian life. But the "program" of most congregations today simply doesn't provide room for such intense disciplines.

The Pentecostals are bound to win out in the spiritual zeal sweepstakes, for they are a selective group. They only attract persons who are interested in making a serious religious commitment; the religious hanger-on doesn't dilute their membership. A regular congregation, however, is a "mass" organization. That is, it takes all comers who will identify with it on some minimal basis. Unfortunately, a large number of people in a typical congregation simply don't want any kind of intense spiritual discipline. They come to church to have their culture-formed attitudes reinforced and to be, in some vague sense, "inspired." Anything that goes beyond or counter to this kind of religiosity to which they have grown accustomed arouses their suspicion and hostility. Since such persons are often the majority in a congregation, it is difficult for that congregation to offer many opportunities for serious spiritual development and living.

However, a broad-based congregation has strengths, too, and this other side of the coin should not be overlooked. As a "mass" organization rather than a selective group, a congregation usually has the kind of stability that helps it to keep functioning over the long haul. We have already noted the various dangers that threaten small groups pursuing with single-minded zeal the truth as they see it. The average congregation contains a greater diversity of views and commitments, but it also tends to carry on after many an intense cell group has burned itself out. Here, too, it may be that the plodding tortoise has something to say to the rabbit who starts off with such a flourish.

Congregations, however, must face the serious challenge of providing within the parish life means for spiritual enrichment and growth of a kind far more intensive than they now offer. Otherwise, their people who seek this sort of thing will have to look elsewhere.

What Is Pentecostalism?

The third attraction of Pentecostalism—the small group fellowship—is one that many congregations had already rediscovered on their own prior to the neo-Pentecostal outburst. For some years now a good number of churches have recognized the value of small groups within the life of the congregation for strengthening Christians in the way of Christ. Informal prayer groups and Bible study groups are regaining their popularity. They provide deep enrichment and strength to the participants, affording them an experience of the Spirit more in keeping with traditional Christianity.

The fourth point—individualized Christianity—if it is an accurate description of Pentecostalism, is an attraction the established church cannot readily offer in the strict sense of the term. Long recognizing that church members generally seek a form of "culture faith" free from the challenging aspects of the gospel, church leaders have worked hard to expand the Christian vision of their members. Denominations and many congregations became deeply involved in the many social struggles of the 1960s. For this effort, they received an unprecedented amount of abuse from the membership, who objected to this form of political and social action. The effort as a whole, however, produced some significant growth in the Christian vision of many church people.

Those clergy and laity who feel most strongly that the church must address itself to the critical issues of society tend to view any movement toward inner spirituality as a step backwards. For example, there was in 1973 a planned promotional evangelism campaign called "Key 73." Officially, it brought together over one hundred denominations to pool their resources in an effort to share the gospel with the nation. Most of the work would be done locally, with support from the national level, including some big rallies and TV specials. As most church people know, "Key 73" turned out to be a fizzle if not a dud. One major contribution to the disaster came from the supporters. Several large denominations only gave lip service to the plans, because a large slice of their clergy felt that "personal evangelism" smacked too much of the "Billy Graham syndrome," meaning concern for "souls" as an excuse for avoiding concern for social justice.

The view that personal Christianity is somehow totally opposed to social Christianity runs deep in the church. Of course the two should be part of the same cloth, but over the years they have not been. It goes without saying that the kind of piety expressed by the Pentecostal movement is not going to satisfy people oriented to social action.

If—and the "if" must be stressed—Pentecostalism is indeed a turn inward from the crucifying challenges of bringing the message of the gospel to social ills, it poses a dangerous threat, an easy way out for too many Christians.

That little "if" gets stress, because there are more optimistic ways to interpret the inward, individualized piety of the Spirit people. Here are two of them.

One claims that nations, like individuals, need time to regroup their thoughts after a period of stress. The recent stress period was the civil and social rights struggles of the sixties which radically transformed our national aspirations and goals. Having gone as far as possible, the nation turns inward to digest what has happened, to discover a new basis for understanding its situation. After a period of readjustment, the nation will be ready for another "great leap forward."

Most social observers say we are now in a period of such reflection and digestion. Our desire to turn inward—find inner peace through psychology or cults, our fascina-

What Is Pentecostalism?

tion with "inner space" after a mind-blowing decade in outer space—has reached epidemic proportions. On this view, the Pentecostal explosion among the middle class churchgoers is but one of several such movements. If we accept this analysis, we would predict that the Pentecostal craze will one day pass. In the meantime, it serves a constructive social purpose, in the sense of helping people settle down to their complex new world by offering a short breathing space.

The second optimistic interpretation of Pentecostal individualism asserts that it supplies a needed corrective to the recent ministry of established churches. Anxious to move people out into the world, these churches interpreted their social ministry in political rather than religious terms. They never quite managed to invest Christian religious symbols with social meaning, so they went directly to political and sociological talk. For example, these churches were unable to convince their members that the symbol "Christ died for the sins of man" includes the redemption of social sins (prejudice, poverty, injustice) as well as personal sins. They had little success giving to the word "salvation" a meaning which included saving the body of man as well as his soul.

As a result, a kind of symbol starvation gripped church people. Familiar symbols of the faith failed to move them or motivate them in the directions they were being called to go. Orin Klapp, in a perceptive book, *The Collective Search for Identity*, makes a strong case for the notion that we are starved for symbols which have enough emotional content to supply what he calls "mystique" to our life. He cites the examples of "patriotism, family, work"—all symbols which once had deep emotional content but which now have been stripped of their power to give meaning to our lives.

Perhaps something of the same process has affected Christian symbols—such as "salvation" or even "Christ." If so, the Pentecostal movement, which uses these symbols and provides an emotional content to go with them, may be feeding the need for satisfying religious symbols.

Of course, the content they are giving to these classic symbols may be ultimately empty, or even false and destructive. But if so, and if this thesis is accepted, it amounts to an urgent call for established churches to find ways to invest these same symbols, familiar to all Christians, with more significant and truly adequate meaning.

We have spent time on this point because it lies at the root of much of the hostility with which established church leaders greet the Pentecostal movement. It is the modern version of the classic collective-continuing versus individual-spontaneous crunch. What is at stake is nothing less than the meaning of what it is to "preach Christ" in today's world.

PENTECOSTAL TEACHINGS

The Pentecostal experience provides many things for its initiates. Some are apparently directly related to the Holy Spirit; others look more sociological or psychological. This same mix holds for Pentecostal teachings as well. If we can describe Pentecostalism by the nature of its experience, we can also describe it by its teachings. When we do, we find that there is a core of uniquely Pentecostal doctrine relating to the gifts of the Spirit. But there is also a set of attitudes toward classic Christian teachings; the latter take on a different flavor because of the doctrine of the gifts. When we combine the specific teachings with the shift in attitudes toward other doctrines, we find that Pentecostalism amounts to an identifiable and distinctive approach to the whole Christian faith.

What Is Pentecostalism?

Let us begin with two distinctive elements in Pentecostal teachings.

1. They believe that being a Spirit baptized Christian is something uniquely different from being a simple Christian.

Traditional Pentecostals view Spirit baptism as a definite experience following upon receiving Christ as savior (either through decision or baptism). They feel almost any Christian can have the experience, which is signalled by the gift of tongues. Bishop O. T. Jones, of the Church of God in Christ, told me that he differs from his brothers on this point. He looks upon a vital, vibrant faith as the true evidence of the Spirit, with or without tongues. Most of his colleagues disagree with him. Neo-Pentecostals in the Protestant churches would lean toward Bishop Jones's position, although they usually stress some form of a definite second experience. Catholic charismatics assert that the Holy Spirit comes in the sacrament of confirmation. They look upon the manifest gifts as expressions of the Spirit already within the confirmand.

Whether a dramatic second experience, or simply a manifestation of the inherent Spirit, the results are the same: a definite expression of the New Testament gifts of the Spirit. Since the normal Christian does not go about speaking in tongues, prophesying, or healing, the Pentecostal is perforce a person set apart. He is a "fulfilled" or "full gospel" Christian. Pentecostals don't say the rest of Christendom is unsaved; they simply assert it is incomplete.

The Pentecostal idea of how the Spirit comes contradicts the teaching of most Protestant churches. These churches feel that the Spirit comes with baptism, that the gifts the Pentecostals cultivate are not the important ones (love being the number one gift), and that the Spirit is present in the community of the faithful at all times. Luther's *Small Catechism* explained the work of the Holy Spirit in terms which Lutherans accept as doctrine, and which other main line churches would agree are sound:

"I believe that I cannot by my own understanding or effort believe in Jesus Christ my Lord, or come to him. But the Holy Spirit has called me through the Gospel, enlightened me with his gifts, and sanctified and kept me in true faith.

"In the same way he calls, gathers, enlightens, and sanctifies the whole Christian Church on earth, and keeps it united with Jesus Christ in the one true faith.

"In this Christian church day after day he fully forgives my sins and the sins of all believers" (*Small Catechism*, Revised Edition).

The focus of the Spirit, in reformation Christianity, is the church of which the believer is a part. His chief blessing is the forgiveness of sins; his main gift, the strength to persevere in Christ's path of loving others. Pentecostalism, in this view, is a side track to nowhere terribly important or interesting.

Before the charismatics moved in, Catholic tradition also taught that the Holy Spirit primarily kept one in blessed union with Christ and his church, providing strength and courage for life in a difficult world.

2. They believe in the reality of the supernatural world.

The supernatural spiritual world of the Bible is heavily populated. On the good side we have the angels, the "cloud of witnesses" (deceased believers), God, Jesus, and so forth. The evil side marshals the forces of Satan, his angels, the "principalities and powers of darkness" and such. Overall, the Bible pictures an active, invisible world

What Is Pentecostalism?

beyond our own. Good and evil forces compete for control of our world, but God's final triumph is assured.

Pentecostals believe this supernatural world is as tangible as our earthly world. This is one point where they and the psychic-spiritualist believers agree.

Most contemporary theology, especially among Protestants, treats this spiritual world, which is so real in the Bible, more as a symbol. We live in the "real" world; the other realm exists, but we see it only through shadowy symbols. You won't, for example, meet many Presbyterians who take angels seriously, or who think of the Devil as a personal, alive tempter and adversary.

But the Pentecostals do. They live in a supernatural world. While they vary as to how one counts the population of this other world, that it is actual reality and that it interacts with our present world goes without question. Among Catholic Pentecostals, for instance, are found a number of theologians identified with Mariology (the doctrines of the heavenly role of Jesus' mother). I heard one Catholic Pentecostal give a "teaching" at a prayer fellowship. She told the community, as a teaching from the Lord, that "Mary is our focus, she is the all in all. The Spirit calls us to unity with Mary."

Protestant Pentecostals won't give Mary such an important role in the supernatural world, but they do offer an important post to Satan. Pentecostal magazines run a host of ads for books about Satan—how he operates, how God is going to wipe him out one day, and how one can fight him and his disciples in the meantime. The Protestant-oriented and fundamentalist neo-Pentecostal magazine *Logos* runs ads for books to help believers release those bound by the occult, which is considered Satan's work.

Odd as this world view appears to a modern rationalist, it is the logical outgrowth of the Pentecostal piety. Accepting the Bible on literal terms means taking this kind of position about the supernatural world. And if one is going to believe in the tangible existence of the Spirit's activities, logically the demonic forces must be given equal play.

In addition to these two characteristic doctrines, the Pentecostals give their special twist to other doctrines accepted by most Christians. Five of these can be noted, and they point out why Pentecostal and non-Pentecostal Christians can often use the same language, but not understand each other.

1. The Pentecostals believe in the literal authority of the Bible and the traditional doctrines derived from it.

In this sense, they are fundamentalistic, although most Catholics are less so because their Pentecost began in the universities. The first step in preparation for the Spirit baptism amounts to believing that God can give it. References are found in the Scriptures. Obviously, the faithful must believe that the Bible is true. The fact that old-line Pentecostals were often rabidly fundamentalist, along with the opposition to the movement by more liberal clergy, helps to emphasize the Bible-believing quality of the movement.

2. They believe God is still active, as the Bible records he was in the past.

Pentecostals do not accept the notion that God is working in some different way now than he did in the earlier centuries. Most Christians, at least in practice, do accept the idea of a different way for God's dealings. A Sunday school teacher told her class, "Yes, Jesus healed people by his touch. But that is because they did not have doctors then. Now we do, and doctors use their knowledge to be God's healers." This woman in effect told her pupils that since man has "come of age," God is demoted to the role of motivator or inspirer, while man does the work. Nonsense, say the Pentecostals. "Praise God for all of modern medicine. But at the same time, don't forget that God healed directly before, and he still does." Once upon a time, some of the early Pentecostals thought going to a doctor or doing anything besides praying for God to heal was the Devil's work. But no more. The human mind, either in medicine or theology, is now quite acceptable, but not at the expense of ignoring God's activity in life.

3. They definitely believe that God is an ongoing presence in life today.

Almost no Christian would dispute this general statement. But Pentecostals truly believe that his presence is as real as the person next to you on the bus. Straight Christians *say* this is true; Pentecostals, with a sometimes obnoxious certainty, *know absolutely* that it is true. It is in this context of the ongoing presence of God that we must see their emphasis on the Holy Spirit. All Christians accept the doctrine of the Holy Spirit. But Pentecostals have made more of it. The Spirit of God, as we noted earlier, is the word picture for God's presence in this world. Certainly their stress on the Holy Spirit is one clear way to emphasize the definite and realizable presence of God here and now.

4. Pentecostals believe that God acts directly.

Conventional Christians, and their churches, also believe in the principle that God acts, but their idea of "direct" is more tangential than the Pentecostals will accept. The regulars claim God acts "through history" as the "Lord of history." He is thus given a huge canvas to work, but it is so big the detail cannot be found. Just where in history does God work now? Aside from a few enthusiastic comments—"God has raised Martin Luther King" or "Senator Goldwater is God's man for the presidency"—which are best attributed to pulpit oratory, the straight Christian cannot put his finger on just where God is working in "history."

Pentecostals avoid this embarrassment. God works directly wherever a Spirit baptized Christian can be found. Pentecostals delight to report how God has directly intervened on their behalf—perhaps to find them a job, or to rescue them from harm in an accident, or to heal their bodies of illness.

The established church believes that God acts through the group, which decides on the ground rules of Bible interpretation and doctrine. The idea of having direct contact with God, which makes the church very dispensable, separates neo-Pentecostals from their denominational colleagues. It has also plagued organizational efforts within the older Pentecostal bodies. The vision of a couple of million people with direct access to God conjures up nightmares of a worse ecclesiastical Tower of Babel than we now endure. The churches who criticize this point in Pentecostal thought have good theological and practical reasons, even if a cynic might see a little fear of someone rocking the boat lurking in the background.

5. They believe that God is a personal God who deals personally.

The intense personal quality of Pentecostal piety is much like that of pietist movements that have come and gone in the church. On the plus side, this sense that God cares deeply for *me* helps make God and his Christ very real. It is nice to be loved in general, but even nicer to

What Is Pentecostalism?

know that lover personally and to be pampered by the lover. No one can honestly say that the run-of-the-mill churchgoer has much of this warm, personal contact with his God.

But we must not ignore the negative side. Put bluntly, inviting God to intervene on behalf of your acne problems, when half the world is hungry, smacks of monumental egotism and lack of personal responsibility. The personal relationship of man to God and vice versa becomes acutely twisted when it focuses exclusively upon the blessing side and ignores the responsibility side. No one likes to hear of responsibility. A recent major study of young people in one large denomination indicated they liked the concepts of love and God's care, but disliked concepts of work. When the denominations finally took steps toward the prophetic voice—which, simply put, has always been a clear call to respond responsibly to God's love by loving others—we could easily expect the exodus from the pews which flowed out toward some other promised land. This is a real issue, one a Christian avoids only at the peril of his authentic faith.

This brief survey of broad Pentecostal doctrines pointed out where they are similar to and different from the traditional churches. While they share much with other Christians, we can safely say that the movement represents a different religious view from the rest of Chrstendom. Whether it is better or worse remains for the individual to decide, but different it is.

CHAPTER SEVEN

THE GIFTS—GOD'S OR MAN'S?

Since Pentecostals differ most sharply and obviously from straight Christians in the way they express their Holy Spirit experience through gifts, it is good to take a look at the major gifts one by one.

Tongues: Tongue speaking, or *glossolalia,* is the best known and most characteristic gift displayed by Pentecostals. It is also the most confusing. Several interpretations of its character have been offered from various quarters.

John Sherrill, editor of the popular religious journal *Guideposts,* explored Pentecostal phenomena in depth from a linguistic point of view, receiving the gift himself in the process. He spent a lot of time recording *glossolalia,* then playing the sounds back to linguists. He was trying to test the theory that speakers in tongues actually articulate a real language, even though it may be unknown to them. He and other Pentecostal writers have collected thousands of testimonies which seem to point to this.

When Sherrill played his recorded tongue speaking to a group of non-Pentecostal linguists, however, he had less spectacular success than the testimonies had warranted. They all agreed that the speech was more than random utterance. It had those structural and rhythmic qualities which are common to all languages—the patterns which separate speech from gibberish. A few caught phrases which "sounded something like" a language they knew. But there the experiment ended.

The Gifts: God's or Man's? 83

I have heard reports claiming someone spoke in "ancient Greek," "ancient Latin," or "old Egyptian." These we can readily doubt, for no one knows for sure how these languages were pronounced. When *glossolalia* is identified as a living tongue, such as Swedish, Chinese, or Arabic, the event is also hard to verify. It is too easy to read more than is actually heard into a sound which is "something like" a familiar language. And the atmosphere of Pentecostal meetings doesn't lend itself to objective study. Sherrill's doubtful linguists were probably right.

Generally, when language identifications are made, the language chosen is one with a liquid sound. Most tongue speaking stresses vowels and soft sounds like "h," while minimizing gutterals such as "g" or explosive sounds such as "b." The sound is melodious and liquid, pitched in a pleasing voice register. In this sense, tongue speech is like singing. Both are free and open vocalizations; both have trouble with gutterals and breath stops.

The other theory connecting *glossolalia* to actual languages claims that the real miracle is a miracle of hearing. The auditor hears his own tongue, but the speaker utters nonsense syllables. This still current explanation arose in the second century, as one way to interpret the events of Acts 2. It escapes testing, for it is entirely too subjective. I can hear what I want to hear, tell you about it—and all you can do is either accept it or call me crazy.

Besides linguistic theories, several psychological hypotheses attempt to explain the phenomenon. One such theory speaks of disassociative speech. People can talk quite differently from their normal pattern. Split personalities, such as "Sybil" who is sixteen different "persons," often change their speech quality, accent, and vocabulary dramatically as they shift from one role to the other.

Another psychological theory is less clinical and more mystical. Dr. Morton Kelsey borrowed it from his teacher, the noted Swiss psychiatrist, Dr. Carl Jung.

Jung holds to the idea of the "collective unconscious." Each one of us stores within our unconscious the whole experience of our race, from primeval man to the present. The content of this collective unconscious emerges in many ways, commonly in our dream life. Tongue speaking, Kelsey speculates, might be a vocal expression of this collective unconscious. It then becomes a divinely given gift by which we express the true language of humanity, drawing upon deeply submerged, unconscious levels of archetypal images. Dr. Kelsey develops this argument, which is rather complex, in his definitive book, *Tongue Speaking*. While clearly the most sophisticated sounding rational explanation to date, we must note that all Jungian thought is based more on intuitive speculations than experimental laboratory research.

Another speculation claims that tongue speaking reveals a human capacity which, like ESP, once belonged to man but which has been lost. In this heyday of "inner space," we willingly believe that many seemingly obscure happenings can, with skill, be duplicated by most people. Some scientific researchers are now pursuing this line of investigation. They expect to discover that tongues manifest a speech power long repressed in man. If they are right, tongue speaking will lose its spiritual uniqueness.

The Gifts: God's or Man's?

Biblical references to *glossolalia* mostly refer to some kind of unintelligible speech, a form of inspired religious utterance. Acts 2 is the chief reference to tongues in the sense of normal language, and this reference might have resulted from a blending of traditions or a confusion by Luke of his sources. In other words, it may have been simple *glossolalia,* to which Luke gave some linguistic reference. He may have done so as the result of a Jewish expectation current in first century circles. The story of the Tower of Babel reveals how man's sin disrupted the oneness of humanity by separating people through diverse languages. In the Golden Age, so the speculation went, man would once again be united by God with a common tongue. This tradition may be found in the obscure *Testament of the Twelve Patriarchs* (Judah 25:3): "And ye shall be for a people of the Lord and *one tongue,* and there shall not be a spirit of deceit of Belial." On this theory, Luke doctored the story of Pentecost to magnify its symbolic value.

Most modern Pentecostals prefer another understanding of tongue speaking. They call it "angelic speech." As one told me, "It is God's own language, given for his praise and adoration."

A woman I will call Janet Nordstad explained it to me this way: "Have you ever been filled with such a desire to praise and glorify God that you run out of words to express your deepest feelings? Many times, I have not had the language at my command to tell my husband how much I love him. Love is like that; it defies our language. So, it isn't at all strange that our human speech fails to adequately express our love and praise of God. When I am praising God, I slip into tongues. It's a beautiful and relaxing experience. The words seem to come without effort. I feel they are truly saying what I feel inside—

even though I don't 'understand them,' they seem to communicate to me. I feel this is God supplying me with the language adequate to his fullest praise."

The big question is whether this speech is the tongue of man or the tongue of angels—or both.

Traditional Pentecostal clergy told me stories about their brethren who have sought the baptism—signified by tongues—for years without success. These sincere people wanted to be sure that when it came, it was the total gift of God. They studiously avoided making any contribution of their own. Their efforts ended in failure. As a matter of pastoral concern, the Pentecostal ministers counsel these seekers to be less fastidious. They should form words on their own, even try to imitate tongues. It will quickly become natural and they will distinctly know the moment. This shift to the "natural" becomes the moment when God's Spirit takes over through baptism.

Catholic charismatics speak quite frankly about human cooperation. In their instruction classes, they teach seekers how to do it. One priest, who has taught tongue speaking to young confirmands, told me: "Any Christian can speak in tongues, theoretically. God does not give this gift to everyone. He divides his gifts among people. But he seems to have spread this gift widely. It is basically a matter of proper teaching. First, the theology, so that the person believes the gift might be his. Then an atmosphere of support, relaxation, and expectancy. Finally, the seeker should start forming words as if he were speaking in tongues. Try this for a while and the results are amazing."

Some Pentecostals report receiving tongues in private. But the group method seems most efficient. The seeker joins a group of Pentecostals. The group balance is watched carefully; no more than a third of the group can be seekers. This insures a general atmosphere of peer pressure toward joining in with the tongues. With this atmosphere, aided by careful teaching and selected Scripture study, surrounded by people who actively want to speak in tongues, and supported by group prayer, the process is much easier.

Some groups set the expectant seeker quietly in a chair in the middle of the room. His friends place their hands upon his head. They pray, often in tongues. Usually the seeker begins to join in, to his amazement and joy. The thrill associated with the first moment of tongue speaking soon wears off, but it remains a pleasant, delightful, usually uplifting experience.

Prophecy: Most folk who stand outside of the Pentecostal circle don't know of this gift. Paul lends it some importance, saying that prophecy, in contrast to *glossolalia,* can be understood and leads to everyone's spiritual growth —not just that of the speaker.

We could term prophecy "intelligible tongues." The speaker appears to undergo the same psychological experience of a tongue speaker, except that his words are coherent—perhaps rapid and a bit breathless, but nonetheless sensible. In Pentecostal circles, believers think of prophecy as a direct revelation from God.

This gift would seem easier to fake than tongues, because anyone can speak normal sentences. But it isn't so simple. The prophecies come out very freely, even from people who normally have trouble expressing themselves. Prophecies habitually come garbed in biblical language; if a hearer doesn't know his Bible well, he could mistake a prophecy for a reading from Scripture. The style of language God chooses apparently relates to the Bible translation used by the prophet. In circles where the King James Bible holds sway, God selects Elizabethan language.

In more progressive Pentecostal groups, the Lord uses the phrase of the New English Bible, the Jerusalem Bible, the New American Standard Version, or even the flat-out colorless idiom of Today's English Version. Sometimes the divine word comes in the harsh phraseology of Ezekiel, and sometimes in the repetitive, simple style of John's charming Gospel. This seems to suggest that the prophecy arises from the unconscious mind of the prophet, who draws upon his favorite biblical writer and translation.

Here are some sample prophecies:

"Repent, I say repent! The day of fire cometh soon. I have given thee a time before the tribulation. Now is the time of salvation. Repent!" This one came from a man at an independent Pentecostal meeting in Los Angeles. When I heard it, the evangelist was in the middle of his sermon. He let the fellow speak, said "Amen! Thank you brother," and went on. Traditionalists such as Assemblies of God people would call this one a false prophecy. It interrupted the flow of the service, contrary to what St. Paul said prophecy should do. One Assemblies pastor told me that when similar things happen in his services, "I tell the Devil to get out of the man. The preaching of God's word should be honored and not interrupted. After you tell a couple of folks to shut up, they don't prophesy that way anymore during sermons. There is a time and place for everything, as Paul makes clear."

A number of prophecies came out of the huge charismatic conference held at Notre Dame in 1973. These have been recorded and dated, then circulated among Catholic charismatics. Here are same samples:

"My people, rejoice in me and again I say rejoice. Open your hearts before me. I have given you my Spirit and my Spirit and your Spirit are an unbeatable combination. I will strengthen you, establish you, settle you, no one shall harm you, and no one can take you out of my arms." In this prophecy, Jesus speaks in the language of John's Gospel, which sounds different than the language chosen by Matthew or Luke. Note the fascinating snatch of modern idiom at the end of the second sentence.

"My children, I am walking among you. I am touching you. I am healing you. I have much more for you to do. But I cannot complete my work until you give everything to me. Everything must come under my Lordship. I love you. I will not fail you. Believe me, I love you. Give it all to me. Continue coming to me as you have come and I will manifest more of my love and my peace among you. Continue coming to me, my people." Like most prophecies which come out of love-oriented Pentecostal groups, in contrast to those with a save-souls slant, this one encourages the Spirit-filled Christian to keep up the good work because there are even more blessings waiting at rainbow's end. The note of total surrender to Jesus characterizes much prophecy.

These prophecies seldom if ever call the group to repent of their racism, or sell all they have for the sake of the poor. Mostly, they encourage the group to continue on the path they have already chosen, only with more zeal and spiritual surrender. These utterances, I should add, are not prophecy in the Jeanne Dixon sense. God does not reveal his future plans in any more detail than the familiar biblical generalities about his ultimate triumph and the creation of a "new heaven and new earth." Most Pentecostals would condemn as false any prophecy which, for instance, predicted the date of a presidential assassination or the hour and place of Jesus' return to earth.

This raises the question of whether every utterance given could gain acceptance as an authentic divine word. The answer is no. The ability to distinguish between true and false prophecy is another gift. Basically, the norm used is Scripture. If the prophecy offered contradicts clear Scriptural teaching, it is *ipso facto* declared false. Sometimes the general consensus of the prayer fellowship provides the corrective. If the majority feel the prophecy offered is not really the word from God, they say so.

Pentecostals, believing in both the heavenly spiritual realm and the unseen forces of darkness, therefore believe that the Devil can use the Spirit gifts for his own sinister purposes. The hapless individual who speaks an unacceptable prophecy finds his group gathered about to pray the Devil from his heart. This could turn out to have grim psychological consequences for the outcast, except that the Spirit groups have a close bond which strongly supports each individual. The Devil, not the person, bears the brunt of their hostility. Though this might seem impossible, it is duplicated in group encounter sessions. These groups sometimes turn on an indiviual with fierce aggressiveness, but when it is over the "victim" remains an accepted member of the group. This is another instance where group dynamics illuminates the working of Spirit fellowships.

For an outsider, a logical question comes to mind: "If prophecy, in the last analysis, isn't going to add or subtract from the totality of what you already believe Scripture teaches, why bother with it?" I asked that of a charming young Catholic charismatic. She replied, "It's more for reassurance. Isn't it wonderful to know that Jesus can still speak to us now, giving us confidence and support?"

Interpretation of tongues: In some ways similar to prophecy, this gift reveals some sharp differences between the traditional Pentecostals and the neo-Pentecostals of Protestantism and Catholicism.

The one blessed with this gift has abilities to interpret the otherwise unintelligible sounds of *glossolalia*. In effect, he is a translator of tongues. As much as tongues itself, interpretation is a direct gift of the Spirit.

In the Assemblies of God churches, members adhere to Paul's advice in the First Letter to the Corinthians as though it were a manual of procedure. Paul says that if a person speaks in tongues in a service, there should always be someone present to interpret it. Otherwise, the tongue speaker should keep silence. Paul preferred rational discourse which edified the whole community. The Assemblies follow Paul's advice closely. They restrain worshipers who speak in tongues for the sake of tongues. Tongue speaking in public worship must be interpreted.

The neo-Pentecostals are much less finicky. They delight in tongues as a vehicle of praise. This is not to say that tongues dominate their meetings. Far from it. Most of the prayer and adoration goes on in normal language, often with a formula overtone given by repeated slogans like "Praise the Lord" or "Thank you, Jesus"—forms of praise also common to non-Pentecostal fundamentalistic groups. But when tongues break forth, neo-Pentecostals don't always insist on interpretation. They accept *glossolalia* as valid in itself.

Why the difference? Are the Assemblies simply more literal about the Bible? One of their pastors told me, "You need to give mature pastoral guidance to the spiritual gifts. Tongues can become so exciting that the believer stops there. We think Paul's advice is sound. We too want to press on toward the higher gifts. We feel that when God speaks through someone it is because he has a message for all to hear—at least in public worship, because that is what worship is all about. So, with Paul, we emphasize the importance of interpretation. They [the neo-Pentecostals] are new at the spiritual gifts. We were too. But we have learned a lot in the last sixty plus years."

Traditional Pentecostals hold that tongues are the

initial evidence of the baptism of the Spirit. Their pastors actively seek to help their people toward the higher gifts. The Assemblies of God people will tolerate uninterpreted tongues if they happen during periods of the service specifically set aside for praise. When an outsider visits one of their services, he might sense an artificial quality to the way tongue speaking stops when the pastor closes the tongue praise with "Amen." It really isn't phoney. It is their way of following St. Paul and striving for both an orderly, uplifting service and the full expression of the gifts of the Spirit.

In practice, interpretation of tongues has about the same content as prophecy and its validity is judged by the same Scriptural norms. The question arises why God might choose this devious two-step approach, rather than electing to communicate through direct prophecy. Pentecostal people simply shrug at this question and point to First Corinthians: "It's in the Bible."

Wisdom: Catholic charismatics talk more about the gift of wisdom than do other Pentecostals. For all practical purposes, wisdom is stillborn prophecy. Teachings from the Lord which do not achieve that hard-to-define community consensus which certifies their divine origin, end up being called wisdom. Remarks made by prayer community members, which help them gain insight into the process of living so intimately with the Spirit, also—if they seem to make sense—gain the status of wisdom. This gift belongs to those who emerge as "teachers," a rather informal process leaning heavily on personal charisma and insight.

Healing: The healing gift is one of the most controversial of the spiritual gifts. No one denies that the Bible records scores of miraculous, God-given healings. But many non-Pentecostal Christians think that "faith healing"

The Gifts: God's or Man's?

is always part of the Pentecostal bag of tricks. Oral Roberts on TV helped reinforce this impression. Spiritual healing—which incidentally is also a big operation among the occult spiritualists—got a black eye from the excesses perpetrated by fraudulent operators who call themselves "faith healers." Serious Pentecostals vigorously object to the term "faith healing." The proper term, they say, is spiritual or divine healing, which implies God as the healing agent. The other implies that one's own faith does the healing. Thus, if God does not grow a leg from your amputated stump, you lack faith. The frauds stress this point because it keeps them out of jail. So long as it is *your* faith and not *their* gifts or skills, they can practice medicine without a license. These frauds often say that going to a doctor reveals a weak faith.

Despite the bad reputation of spiritual healing in the past, a goodly number of non-Pentecostal Christians enthusiastically believe that God can intervene beyond the normal medical process to effect a dramatic healing. Dr. Norman Vincent Peale, not himself a Pentecostal, speaks of the close relationship between a strong vital spiritual life and a healthy physical body. A few thousand doctors agree with him. Recent developments showing how attitudes affect bodily health have cast a whole new light on the notion of faith healing. The Order of St. Luke the Physician is a very sober Episcopalian group dedicated to divine healing. St. Stephen's Church in Philadelphia has engaged in a major healing ministry since the mid-1950s. They do this without getting on the Pentecostal train, using spiritual healing as an *adjunct* to medicine.

Though neo-Pentecostals are more cautious about the gift, traditional Pentecostals believe strongly in spiritual healing. The healing ministry of the Assemblies of God is guided by James 5:14–16, where the writer gives directions for spiritual healing. Basically, James says the elders should pray over the sick man and anoint him with oil. This ritual is then supported by the fervent prayers of the whole community. James underscores the relationship of forgiveness of sins (God's grace) and healing, rather than speaking in strictly Holy Spirit language: "The prayer offered in faith will save the sick man, the Lord will raise him from his bed, and any sins he may have committed will be forgiven. Therefore confess your sins to one another, and pray for one another, and then you will be healed" (vv. 15–16). In the Gospels Jesus' healings are often interpreted as signs of God's graceful forgiveness as well as wonders done by God.

Following James's advice, an Assemblies pastor, joined by a couple of his elders, will visit the sick, pray for them, and anoint them with oil. The whole congregation also prays for the sick. The pastors I spoke with report that they have seen enough signs of divine intervention in healings to keep their confidence up in the truth of James's instructions.

The contemporary star in the healing firmament is a lady, the Reverend Kathryn Kuhlman. She belongs to the Evangelical Church Alliance, one of our lesser known denominations. And she is not a devoted Pentecostal. In fact, she says, in reference to the gift of healing: "I would never say that I have received any gift. I am leery of folks who boast of this or that gift. My purpose is the salvation of souls. Divine healing is secondary to the transformation of a life."

Kathryn Kuhlman has a refreshingly sober view of her task. Unlike some healers who overflow with confidence in their powers, she says, "It is not a thrilling responsibility, but awesome, and sometimes so awesome I wish I had never been called to this part of the ministry." She frankly

The Gifts: God's or Man's?

admits, "I have no healing virtue. I have no healing power. I am absolutely dependent upon the power of the Holy Spirit."

Other gifts: The list of gifts is a long one indeed. Of St. Paul's compilation in 1 Corinthians 12, we note that a few gifts still remain. Putting "the deepest knowledge into words" is easy enough to understand. "Faith," for Paul as well as his orthodox followers, is also a gift from God. "Miraculous powers" is a grab bag rubric which covers almost anything. It is a bit too general for the Pentecostals. Sheer wonder working, they would say, comes too close to the satanic for comfort. This is an area best left alone, for it requires still another gift: "the ability to distinguish true spirits from false." Living in their shadowy world of wondrous events, Pentecostals always find themselves trying to separate God's work from the Devil's. This gift of discernment unfortunately is as rare in their circles as in the general run of human affairs.

What about the highest gift, love? As we said earlier, we can best leave the judgments on this to each individual. One observation is in order, however: most Pentecostals I spoke with told me they found more love in the Spirit fellowship than in their churches. They gave clear testimony to how the Spirit was helping them grow in love. Most of them spoke of love in terms of personal relationships, such as coming to love a neighbor who was once hated, or developing a passion for the "unsaved." Very few spoke of an enlarged love for humanity in the sense of a burning compassion for and commitment to social justice. But then, neither do most regular Christians. Pentecostals feel that the love they find in Pentecostalism, however it may be evaluated by those who are outside the movement, beats what they used to know before their Spirit baptism.

CHAPTER EIGHT

WILL THE FIRE BUILD OR BURN?

Renewal movements in the church come and go, but never cease. Montanus viewed his movement as God's force for renewal. The modern interest in fresh liturgies and meaningful theologies expresses renewal in other ways. In a real sense, the church never really "arrives." So long as it is God's colony in the midst of human frailty, it must keep striving, constantly renewing itself. Is the Pentecostal explosion a dynamic force for church renewal?

Right now the new Pentecostalism spells trouble more often than renewal. Congregations split, pastors get fired, friends separate over the issue of spiritual gifts. That is a sorry role for the gift of love. Part of the blame rests on the neo-Pentecostals. Sometimes obnoxiously zealous, they tend to condemn their brethren instead of guiding them in love toward the "higher truth." And no small part of the blame goes to the established churches, who display the expected distaste for zealots who disturb the normal course of events.

In addition, Pentecostals raise some tricky doctrinal problems which obstruct their plans for renewal. Traditional Pentecostal churches hold that Spirit baptism is a definite second experience, following upon salvation. This second baptism is marked by the sign of tongues. Few established churches can buy that, for they hold that the Spirit comes with water baptism or, in the case of Roman Catholics, with the sacrament of confirmation. Pentecostals stand little chance of getting churches to rewrite basic doctrine. But the neo-Pentecostals are already making accommodations as they adjust their Spirit experience to the context of their denomination. This may one day lead to a divorce in the present honeymoon relationship between neo-Pentecostals and the traditional Pentecostals, but it would lead to a closer relationship with established churches.

This crisis situation may ease in time. Already, signs of increased maturity appear on both sides. One non-Pentecostal pastor in Hawaii works with a church council and leadership who are heavily charismatic. They get along well. The people were well into the Pentecostal experience at the time they called him as their pastor. Both sides accepted their differences. They manage to love each other. The pastor frankly admits that his Pentecostal members show more zeal and enthusiasm for ministry than the others. He and his Pentecostals spend a lot of time in study, helping each other with their insights while respecting each other as authentic Christians. Their happy experience isn't duplicated everywhere, but it does show a path toward a more promising future relationship between the two groups.

The compromise twist to the classic Pentecostal view is this: the manifest gifts of the Spirit belong to every Christian. Coming to exercise these gifts, by speaking tongues and the like, is not a "second baptism." It is merely the unfolding of the Spirit already within. Catholic charismatics pioneered this compromise position. Already, in some dioceses, the catechisms used to instruct the youngsters for confirmation teach spiritual gifts as part of the blessings to come from God when they are confirmed. One priest told me, "We view charismatic gifts as the unfolding of the power of the Spirit which is given to us all."

The Lutheran Charisciples, a Seattle based group of Lutheran Pentecostals who have a network of several hundred professional church workers, put their version of this compromise position this way: "Acknowledging and accepting Jesus not only as 'Savior' but also as living and unchanging Lord now permits the *already indwelling Holy Spirit* in the believer to be 'released' into one's total being and daily life (1 Pet. 1:2). Thus, one *consciously accepts* and *confirms his 'Spirit baptism.'*

"Such a spiritual contract between the *serious Christian* and his Lord *generally results* in the 'anointing' with Christ's love-gift, namely, the praising and praying 'in tongues' " (Acts 19:6, emphases mine).

Note how this compromise wording says the Spirit is "already indwelling" and his expression is "generally"—but not always!—manifest in the gift of tongues. This kind of thinking may pave the way for further theological dialogue with Lutheran leaders. However, it should be made clear that the Lutheran church, like most old Protestant churches, offers no doctrinal basis for and has no tradition of speaking in tongues. Besides, even in the compromise wording there crops up the little term "serious Christian." This suggests that those not with Pentecost are not "serious." That is the stumbling block. How can you dialogue with people who will not accept you as a "serious Christian" unless you agree with them?

In the final analysis, accepting noncharismatic Christians as completely authentic and fulfilled believers may be more of a compromise than the Pentecostals can endure. To do so would mean they lose their main thrust, renewal. Renewal needs someone to renew; it has to find "sorry Christians" to work on or it has no purpose. There are plenty of them around to work on, but they usually don't care enough about Christ even to listen to a Pentecostal. So, the charismatics go to work on those believers who are trying seriously to apply faith to life, but who do

Will the Fire Build or Burn?

not speak in tongues. Calling these people "unfulfilled" usually leads to confrontation and conflict.

However, if the charismatics approach their task differently, it is quite possible that they will be able to effect a renewal within the church, both in terms of recovering the basic Christian symbols and in providing a satisfying emotional content to go with them. Some denominations, noting the large numbers who defect to Pentecostal ranks, may turn to the charismatics for help in enriching the cultic and symbolic lives of their faithful. These denominations would then respond to dimensions of the Christian faith which, in parish practice and national policy, they have often ignored. This could lead to a rekindling of personal faith and piety in the established churches. If so, a necessary element of renewal would flourish. But the total picture of church renewal embraces far more than enriched personal piety.

If the Pentecostal movement matures along lines an optimistic observer can already see emerging, it may direct the Spirit-filled energy of believers into wider channels. Because Pentecostalism has acquired a theological stance historically associated with personal salvation Christianity, we might doubt that it would ever move into the larger social dimensions of faith. But there is obviously no theoretical reason why a Spirit-filled movement cannot reach into the wider aspects of human justice.

Pentecostals have already begun to penetrate into the nitty-gritty of human life. Consider the Reverend Dave Wilkerson and his Teen Challenge organization. This group works with drug addicts in the urban ghettos. Their record is rather good; somewhat better in fact than the federal rehabilitation programs. Pentecostal religious experiences seem to offer good substitutes for drugs. Pentecostals also have an historic identification with the oppressed and downtrodden. If their social theology outgrows the "pie in the sky when you die" business, they might end up the most potent ecclesiastical force for social change among the oppressed classes.

Pentecostalism also holds promise for breaking down the persistent racism which erodes Christianity. On the surface, Pentecostal denominations are split black and white. These color line churches evolved because society demanded it. Back in 1906, the Azuza Street revival brought blacks and whites to the same church. Founders of both black and white Pentecostal denominations received the same Spirit in the same place. Pentecostal gatherings show more racial integration than most other churches. *Look* magazine some years ago reported that the fullest, most spontaneous integration in the South happened at Pentecostal meetings. An observer will often see black and white people hugging each other and sharing their tearful joy, something not often found in other churches. Pentecostals include a large percentage of blacks, chicanos, and Puerto Ricans; they are already more integrated than many denominations. An emotional, transcendent experience welds diverse people together—at least for the moment. If Pentecostals can bring this interracial fellowship out of the meeting onto the streets, they will do infinite good for the Christian church.

No one can absolutely assert that these potentials will ever be actualized. My intention is simply to make it clear that it can happen. Non-Pentecostals should recognize the promising elements inherent in the Pentecostal experience.

Within the major denominations, Pentecostals can either bring about a rupture, or spearhead a renewal. I suspect the latter will occur among the Catholic charismatics. They remain close to the cultic life of their church, participate with renewed vigor in the Mass and other sacraments—

Will the Fire Build or Burn?

besides adding new qualities of fellowship and service through their paraparochial prayer groups.

Catholic charismatics put heavy stress on community. Many Protestant groups have followed their lead. Pentecostal communities are being formed. These are not to be confused with the youth culture communes of the Children of God and other "Jesus freaks." The Pentecostal communities draw regular middle class folk, who may buy homes adjacent to each other or share the same quarters. They seek to share a more intimate Christian fellowship. Some of them, like the Word of God community, host other Pentecostals from time to time. These communities become centers of strength for the movement, much as monasteries were for the church in the early Middle Ages.

Father Dennis Bennett, the Episcopalian priest who became one of the early celebrities of the movement, cautions Pentecostals to stay within the church structures. He emphasizes how the Pentecostal experience can give meaning and reality to the liturgy of the church. He tells how he cried with emotion for the first time during the service after he received the Holy Spirit. If Pentecostals use their new Spirit to enrich their churches, they may well become God's agents for renewal.

However bright or dark one wants to paint the possible futures for the movement in relationship to established Christianity, no hypothetical scenario will mean much to those who are caught in the throes of the Pentecostal controversy. What can they do in the present moment, when the issue is still clouded and hotly debated?

The following points might be helpful.

First, be willing to look for the positive aspects of the Pentecostals' experience. You may not not agree with the step they have taken, but the fact that they made the move tells you something. They found in Pentecostalism what they did not find in normal church life. Discuss this carefully. Look for the underlying dynamic beneath the surface practice. For example, the act of speaking in tongues may fill an honest need for divine praise which the parish does not supply. Again, their discovery of deeply personal meanings in Scripture through a Pentecostal fellowship may suggest that the historical-critical approach commonly used in many parishes doesn't have enough existential guts for such a person.

Second, don't condemn the pride of the newly baptized Pentecostal until you are very sure that you are not threatened. Few things threaten a Christian—professional or nonprofessional—more than a fellow believer who is happier, more active, and more responsive than he is. Much of the irrational heat in the Pentecostal dialogue stems from the traditional believer's sense of unconscious threat. If a Pentecostal, turned on to personal evangelism, tries to persuade you that this is the core and center of authentic Christianity, you can doubtless marshal some arguments to rebut him. But when you are plagued with guilt because you have not personally borne witness to your faith in twenty years, your reactions become irrationally hostile. In other words, with a modest sense of Christian love, be willing to learn from the Pentecostal. They are not complete idiots and you are not a perfect saint.

Third, consult mature Pentecostals for help. I spoke with one pastor who was at his wits end trying to cope with a group of charismatics in his congregation. I suggested he seek counsel from an Assemblies of God pastor or a charismatic Catholic priest. He looked stunned. "Are you crazy?"

The simple fact is that Pentecostals know a lot more about both the blessings and the freaky side of Spirit experiences than the outsider. And they are usually willing to help. Perhaps pastors fear sheep stealing, but I suspect this fear is overblown. I spoke with one Assemblies pastor who is probably typical of the matured generation of Pentecostals, although he is rather young in years. His father was also an Assemblies pastor, which gives him long experience in the movement. If pastoral wisdom and skill happen to be a Spirit gift, he has it. He said he is more than willing to aid other clergy who cannot handle the Pentecostal explosion.

"My first concern," he told me, "is for salvation. If people belong to a church which preaches the path of salvation through Christ's atonement—which includes most churches if they preach what their doctrine states—I certainly am not going to 'steal sheep.' But I am also interested in the baptism of the Spirit. I think I have a lot of experience with this. I know its blessings, but I also know its excesses and problems. Sometimes, in that first flush of Pentecost, a person gets overly aggressive. I know this reaction, and I can help counsel them on the proper stewardship of the spiritual gifts.

"I have helped some congregations with Pentecostals in their midst come to the point where they help each other and build up the Body of Christ. The Spirit should bring greater love and harmony. I know that in some situations the differences are too sharp, but this is certainly not always the case."

Catholic Pentecostals I spoke with indicated the same willingness to help. Pentecostalism is, in itself, a kind of ecumenical movement. For all the differences among Pentecostals, they share a common and delightful spiritual experience. When working with various denominations, they appear willing to help the charismatic understand his experience within the light of his own theology. Naturally, some Pentecostals will eagerly sweep away any sheep they can, but this can be said of certain ministers in other groups as well. The point is that there are many skilled and spiritually mature people who know a lot more about Pentecostalism than you do, and their help is worth seeking out.

Fourth, be open to the Spirit yourself. The Spirit moves in diverse and wondrous ways, so this advice should not be taken as necessarily buying into the Pentecostal movement. However, Pentecostals do proclaim, rightly or wrongly, an aspect of the faith which main line churches have long ignored. If you cannot accept their manifestations of the Spirit, at least be prepared to look inside yourself for other expressions of the Spirit. In an open dialogue, perhaps you can learn something about yourself and grow in the Spirit along lines more congenial to your own style of Christianity.

Fifth, don't panic if you have a few defections. Once, a television network yanked a "Gunsmoke" episode off the air because it received four hundred negative letters, out of an estimated audience of four million. This kind of overreaction also infects churches. Five people leave a congregation over the Pentecostal issue and the whole congregation pushes the panic button. Sure, some Pentecostals simply won't feel at home in some Presbyterian, Baptist, Lutheran, or Episcopalian churches. But many of them will, with wise counseling. A group like the Southern Baptists, whose doctrinal position does not tolerate tongues, has to kick out their charismatics. Other denominations have a range of options; they need not jump on separation right away.

Sixth, learn something about Pentecostalism. This means reading material which is both pro and con. But even more, it means associating with Pentecostals. Seeing people directly, talking with them and knowing them, leads to clearer insight than a thousand books on the ins and outs of the doctrine. You can find charismatic fellowships nearly every-

Will the Fire Build or Burn?

where. It is a loose movement, so you might have to ask around. If you indicate you are sincerely interested and come with a positive attitude, they will gladly receive you. Plan to attend more than one meeting. Initially you may be shaken a bit by what you see—the first time you hear tongues it can be a trifle unnerving. When you go back again and again, you can properly look beneath the surface to discover the real reasons the movement exists. Talk to the people; evaluate their testimonies. You may end up with a firm conviction that what they have is not for you, but at least you will come away with a few things which deeply impress you and will help you grow in your own grasp of Christ.

The divisiveness associated with Pentecostalism seems most prominent in the Protestant neo-Pentecostal circles. Catholic charismatics manage to feel at home in their church body. It may help Protestants to realize that tearing a church apart over this issue is not necessarily inevitable.

Even before the Pentecostals appear in your midst, you can learn something from their experience. Basically, they are happy because they have found, at a satisfying emotional level, a religious experience which gives a flesh and blood, personal reality to their faith. They find a mystique. How much is this emotional side of man's religious needs cultivated in your parish? If this need is met in terms of both theology and practice, people have no need to search elsewhere for it. It's that simple.

People need a satisfying mystique in order to move ahead in life. Socially concerned Christians, who object to the overly personal style of Pentecostal faith, and who seldom think mystique is important, should take this seriously. They dismiss it as "pietism." Far from it; too many expressions of our social responsibility amount to what activists call a "head trip"—empty ideologies, sterile rationality. Maybe wrapping our social efforts in the language of the Christian symbol system would help, clearly relating the need for social justice to the biblical language. When church members complain about too much politics from the pulpit, they *may* really mean that they object to hearing these ideas expressed from a pulpit in current political vocabulary and imagery.

One of the most active, creative, and responsive congregations in the field of social action has learned this lesson well. They begin each project with Bible study and serious theological reflection. They ask, "Why should a Christian do this?" When they find the answer they adopt the social program into their mystique and move out with energy. This is a conservative, evangelical Baptist church, yet its efforts result in action and not just talk. One measure of its commitment is this: the congregation voted to mortgage its paid-up property for $300,000 to finance programs for social change and human betterment.

Many churches have tried to stimulate spirituality by freshening up their worship services. The results of this "liturgical renewal" are mixed. A priest, reflecting on the liturgical renewal movement that hit his denomination after Vatican II, told me, "The trouble with liturgical renewal is that it changes the form and not the content. You can't impose a celebration style of worship on people who find no inner joy in the faith. But once they find this personal joy, the new style of worship comes naturally."

Helping people find joy in their faith involves more than sending up balloons at worship, or slipping a few touchy-feely sensitivity training gimmicks into the service. It involves deep reflection on the faith and spiritual growth through rediscovering the depths of God's marvelous mercy.

One effective means for this is the small group Bible study. Using an approach which examines the historical background of the passage and engages in Socratic dialogue to apply its meaning to each person, "existential" Bible study has a record of helping people find renewed spirituality. It involves people directly and takes advantage of the dynamics of small groups for personal growth. In the long run, this kind of renewal will probably go farther than any changes in worship form, or exercising spectacular "gifts." Talking to Pentecostals, I suspect that what they found in their Spirit fellowships could also be found in these kinds of spiritual growth groups.

If congregations can energize the power of Christian symbols, if Christians can recognize that not every believer wants a "head faith," if pastors trained in long disciplines of rationality can grasp the simple emotional needs of most people, and if Christians will stop making personal and corporate faith two totally different things—well, should all these ifs come to pass, we could all celebrate the coming of the new Pentecost.

The Spirit moves mightily through the church in wonderfully varied ways. The Pentecostals don't have exclusive rights to his services. Unless, of course, the rest of us let them.